D0790847

ON
ISLAM

DISCARDED

DISCARDED

ON ISLAM

Muslims and the Media

Edited by
ROSEMARY PENNINGTON
and HILARY E. KAHN

INDIANA UNIVERSITY PRESS

This book is a publication of

Indiana University Press
Office of Scholarly Publishing
Herman B Wells Library 350
1320 East 10th Street
Bloomington, Indiana 47405 USA

iupress.indiana.edu

© 2018 by Indiana University Press

All rights reserved

No part of this book may be reproduced or
utilized in any form or by any means, electronic
or mechanical, including photocopying and
recording, or by any information storage and
retrieval system, without permission in writing
from the publisher.

The paper used in this publication meets the
minimum requirements of the American National
Standard for Information Sciences—Permanence
of Paper for Printed Library Materials, ANSI
Z39.48-1992.

*Manufactured in the
United States of America*

Library of Congress
Cataloging-in-Publication Data

Names: Pennington, Rosemary, editor. | Kahn,
    Hilary E., editor.
Title: On Islam : Muslims and the media / Edited
    by Rosemary Pennington and Hilary E. Kahn.
Description: Bloomington, Indiana : Indiana
    University Press, [2018] | Includes
    bibliographical references and index.
Identifiers: LCCN 2017034239 (print) | LCCN
    2017032898 (ebook) | ISBN 9780253032560
    (e-book) | ISBN 9780253029348 (cloth : alk.
    paper) | ISBN 9780253032553 (pbk. : alk. paper)
Subjects: LCSH: Islam in mass media. |
    Muslims—Public opinion. | Islam—Customs
    and practices.
Classification: LCC P96.I84 (print) | LCC P96.
    I84 O5 2018 (ebook) | DDC 070.4/49297—
    dc23
LC record available at https://lccn.loc.
    gov/2017034239

1 2 3 4 5   23 22 21 20 19 18

Redford Township District Library

3 9009 0018 8633 8

CONTENTS

MUSLIM VOICES

CRASH COURSE IN ISLAM

ACKNOWLEDGMENTS

THIS VOLUME IS THE CULMINATION of a decade of work examining and challenging the representation of Islam and Muslims in media. Launched by Indiana University's Center for the Study of Global Change with support from the Social Science Research Council in 2008, the Voices and Visions of Islam and Muslims from a Global Perspective project worked to reframe the public understanding of Islam and Muslim life. This work was only made possible through support from and collaboration with our many partners, both at Indiana University and elsewhere. Among those partners are the staff of Indiana Public Media, including executive director Perry Metz, director of digital media Eoban Binder, and former producer Annie Corrigan. No longer with the outlet but still vital to the success of the project were Adam Schweigert, Christina Kuzmych, Cary Boyce, Liz Leslie, Megan Meyer, and Scott Witzke. The Center for the Study of Global Change relied on a number of Indiana University partners, including the African Studies Program, East Asian Studies Center, Inner Asian and Uralic National Resource Center, Russia and East European Institute, Institute of European Studies, Center for the Study of the Middle East, Muslim Student Association, Media School, and School of Global and International Studies.

We worked hard to create partnerships not only at the university, but also in the larger community. Our collaborations with the Islamic Center of Bloomington, Bloomington Area Arts Council, and Monroe County Public

Library helped make the project, and therefore this volume, stronger. We are also indebted to the Muslim Alliance of Indiana as well as the Islamic Society of North America for their support of this project.

We are, of course, thankful for the contributions of our advisory board to the project. Their thoughtful feedback and suggestions helped ensure that our scope remained broad and that we produced a mosaic of perspectives on Islam. Our board members are Asma Asfaruddin, Cigdem Balim, Gardner Bovingdon, Shakeela Hassan, Zaineb Istrabadi, Kevin Jaques, Ed Lazzerini, Christine Ogan, Janet Rabinowitch, Faiz Rahman, and Nazif Shahrani. The late Elsa Marston, activist and author, was also an active and dedicated board member. Program officer Tom Asher at the Social Science Research Council was quite helpful during the initial years of our project.

A special thank you goes out to the hosts of our podcasts, Manaf Bashir and Steve St. George. To listen to other podcasts about Islam and Muslim life beyond those in this book, visit the Voices and Visions website, www .muslimvoices.org.

ESSAYS

THE VISION BEHIND MUSLIM VOICES

Hilary Kahn

LARGE SWATHS OF THE GENERAL public only encounter Islam and Muslims in news stories when something tragic or terrifying happens, such as the 2017 attacks in London and Istanbul and the 2016 Orlando nightclub shooting. The representation of Muslims in these stories often portrays them as radicalized, irrational, and uncontainable terrorists or depicts their suffering in a desensitized and inhumane way. While a story will occasionally be found in which Muslims are humanized or their faith contextualized, the typical narrative people find in news media is one that distances Islam and Muslims, decontextualizes the faith and its believers, misrepresents the religion as a security risk, and presents a community that is, quite simply, *not us*. This portrayal was shockingly exemplified in the 2015 story of Ahmed Mohamed, a Texas teenager who was disciplined by his school because he took parts of a digital clock to school. He was handcuffed and arrested by police and charged with taking a "hoax bomb" to school. It was suggested that Mohamed was disciplined and arrested because he was a *Muslim* and, therefore, suspect.

This is and always has been unacceptable, but the current onslaught of misrepresentations of Islam and Muslims is quite possibly more terrifying than the images in news media themselves. The perpetuation of such a framing is helping build impenetrable walls of indifference, dread, and fatigue, which prevent human responses of concern, connection, or even a willingness to learn. Examples of these ideological boundaries being fortified by the media abound. Muslim leaders are all potential terrorists, such as Abu Bakr al-Baghdadi being depicted as the face of Islam.[1] In 2015, police initially refused to define the horrific shooting of three Muslim students in Chapel Hill, North Carolina, as a hate crime, instead diminishing it to a parking dispute. The press did not question this analysis and instead represented the incident as an isolated crime by a self-proclaimed bigot rather than being part of a larger systemic hatred and fear of Muslims.

American politics, of course, also has a role to play in the building of walls of indifference and distrust. During the US presidential election in 2016, then candidate Donald Trump claimed that Ghazala Khan, the mother of war hero Captain Humayun Khan, who was killed in a car bombing while serving in Iraq in 2004, did not speak at the Democratic National Convention because, as a Muslim woman, she was prevented from speaking in public. Criticizing a "Gold Star Family" is unheard of in American politics, and the assumption that Mrs. Khan's silence at the convention was a sign of religious gender oppression rather than motherly grief quite simply would not have occurred had the family not been Muslim. Trump was among those who questioned whether President Barack Obama was legally allowed to hold that office, suggesting he was not a native-born United States citizen. This "birther" debate was wrapped up in race and religion, and a number of Americans believed (and still do) that Obama is a secret Muslim. The press did little to push back at this idea until former secretary of state Colin Powell worked to discredit it during an appearance on NBC's *Meet The Press* program.

Social media is ripe with a range of depictions of Islam, from the humane to the hateful. In March 2017, Twitter was filled with tweets using the hashtag #MuslimWomensDay. Launched by a Muslim activist known as the Muslim Girl, the hashtag was designed to start a conversation about the everyday lives and experiences of Muslim women. The hashtag found its way into other social media spaces, such as Tumblr, Facebook, and Instagram as Muslims shared stories of their lives. But it took only a few hours before people began using the #MuslimWomensDay hashtag to share Islamophobic or anti-Muslim ideas—some of them wrapped in a frighteningly violent rhetoric. It was a visible reminder of how vitriolic the debate over Islam in the West has become in all media, and how quickly affinity shifts to revulsion.

The distancing in politics and in news media makes it difficult to create moments of empathy or compassion for Muslim suffering because all Muslims are treated as the enemy. All Muslims, teenage clock makers or not, are suspect. One can turn a blind eye to Syrian refugees or families remaining in war-torn Syria, since they are discursively conflated with Muslim security risks; that is, until a photo of a motionless child killed by chemical weapons in the arms of a wailing parent somehow penetrates the wall of indifference. It is *this* power to lessen the distance between ourselves and those we see as threatening that lies in the hands of journalists and media practitioners, and it is the potential use of this influence that is the underlying reason why this volume exists. The news media has the responsibility to dissect these narratives and provide more humane and contextualized understandings of Islam and Muslims. Journalists have the potential to dramatically change public sentiment and understanding, but they too need more information, more engagement with Islam and Muslims, and some practical and scholarly frameworks to put this accountability into action.

This responsibility and ability to rescript the narratives around Islam and Muslims comes at no better time. Tides of anti-immigrant, antidifference, anti-Islam, and antiglobalism sentiment are swelling, and a public response of exclusion and nationalism is a global and complicated issue that itself requires more nuanced understanding. As real and ideological walls are being constructed and fortified through policies, metal fencing, and disdain, this volume marks a critical moment for the news media and its commitment to providing accurate and meaningful information for the general public. This, of course, is complicated by the networked world we live in, one in which social media can be used to circulate stories of Muslim life while, at the same time, circulate fake news about the way Muslims plan to flood the West in a tidal wave, leaving sharia and oppression in their wake.

We aim to help journalists and media scholars become more familiar with Islam and its believers and to provide best practices and scholarly contexts to reporting on Islam and Muslim lives. We recognize, however, that knowledge is not enough. What matters to us is what our readers will do with the information and stories they encounter in this volume. We hope this book provides media practitioners and scholars with the skills, knowledge, and attitudes they need to tackle the harmful misunderstandings about Islam that permeate public sentiment. This has always been part of our responsibility and one that we now share with you.

This volume emerged from Indiana University's Voices and Visions: Islam and Muslims from a Global Context Project, funded by the Social Science Research Council's Academia in the Public Sphere Program and housed in the IU Center for the Study of Global Change. Through the creation of podcast and video series, social media accounts, webchats, blogs, discussion forums, resources, and academic writing, we created a space where issues and ideas about Islam were debated, often vigorously, by non-Muslims and increasingly by Muslims. The project explored the diversity of Islam and tackled the harmful climate of misunderstanding about Muslims that had heightened in the aftermath of 9/11.

In 2011, we hosted the Re-Scripting Islam Conference. It featured a diverse range of media practitioners and scholars, whose presentations have become the basis of this book. To frame the essays now in this volume, we asked the authors to write about their research and experience with Muslims or Islam and the media. This broad prompt allowed each author to enter into the subject matter from his or her own involvement and understanding and to distill lessons and best practices in reporting on Muslims and their faith. This mix of voices—television producers, social media editors, lawyers, media commentators, print reporters, and professors of communication, media, religion, and the humanities—also represents multiple regional perspectives and consists of both Muslims and non-Muslims. We feel strongly that this is a conversation for Muslims and non-Muslims. And, being non-Muslim ourselves, we have become very aware of the need for this conversation and the delicate balance this discussion perpetuates. This has never been a matter of speaking for or even about. This is simply a conversation that we have a responsibility to facilitate but never to direct. Our biggest contribution to this dialogue is that we continue to invite many voices, scholarly and nonscholarly, Muslim and non-Muslim, and from all over the world, to participate.

Alongside the essays in this volume, the diversity of perspectives and our goals of public scholarship are sustained through the inclusion of transcriptions of Indiana University's Voices and Visions productions: *Muslim*

Voices and *Crash Course in Islam*. *Muslim Voices* podcasts represent human experiences and allow access to academic and personal understanding readers might not otherwise encounter. *Crash Course in Islam* provides an accessible introduction to some of the basic tenets of Islam. *On Islam*'s mix of essays, voices, and information reflects our commitment to public scholarship that promotes not only knowledge but also empathy, skills, and action. Our expectation is that this volume will find its way into newsrooms, living rooms, and classrooms by offering standards of media practice, diverse public and academic perspectives, research and critical scholarship on representations of Islam and Muslims, contextualized understanding about Islam, and insight into the diversity of Muslim lives.

As we look back at a decade of work, we recognize our work is far from over. Islamophobia is on the rise, as are the negative and stereotyped media portrayals of Muslims and Islam. The need for an understanding of the factors leading to those portrayals, as well as for guidelines to help improve the representation of Islam and Muslims, is greater than ever. In fact, sometimes it seems as if little has improved. This critical moment calls for us to double down on our original commitment and consider new approaches and audiences.

We thus invite you to join the conversation. Read the essays, learn about Islam, encounter personal insights into Muslim lives, and explore the practical and theoretical contexts of reporting on Islam. In so doing, help us conquer stereotypes, challenge ideological walls, and promote more meaningful and accurate understanding. We hope you will create spaces and narratives where plural opinions matter and where there is a sustained commitment to creating globally engaged and educated citizens. Please use the voices and perspectives in this volume to develop new knowledge, a more nuanced understanding about Islam and Muslims, and a keener sense of responsibility. Most importantly, act on this information, pierce a few stereotypes, challenge some conceptual walls, and make a difference in newsrooms, ivory towers, and far beyond.

Hilary Kahn is Director of the Voices and Visions Project, Assistant Dean for International Education and Global Initiatives, and Director of the Center for the Study of Global Change in the School of Global and International Studies at Indiana University. She is author of *Seeing and Being Seen: The Q'eqchi' Maya of Guatemala and Beyond* and editor of *Framing the Global: Entry Points for Research* (IUP).

ONE

REFLECTING ON MUSLIM VOICES

Rosemary Pennington

Slammed Doors and Hot Sun

It was a hot August day in southern Indiana. I had spent much of the afternoon haunting parking lots and sidewalks, trying to get strangers to talk to me. As the sweat poured down my back and forehead, I grew increasingly aggravated. At some point in their careers, most reporters will be forced to collect MOS, what we call the "Man on the Street" perspective. I've been reporting since I was nineteen; I've collected MOS on just about every topic under the sun. AIDS, movies, politics, beer. You name it, I've probably asked someone's opinion about it. I've had people refuse to talk to me, and I've had people talk my ear off. Nothing, though, could have prepared me for what I experienced that day in a small Indiana town.

I should back up and say that I don't think what happened that afternoon is so much a reflection on that particular town as it is a reflection on how little average Americans know about Islam or Muslims. Muslims have been living in the United States since before it was actually a country, but their religion was overshadowed by the politics of race and slavery. Ed Curtis does a great job of explaining how early Islam became wrapped up in the popular American imagination with "native" African religions and so was not really visible in the United States until late.[1] And when it became visible, it was associated with "others," with people from someplace else, someplace dark and foreign and scary. This was happening while the Muslim population in America continued to grow.

And still we know so little about Islam or Muslims. Unfortunately, it wasn't until after the September 11th attacks that Americans began to feel a need to understand the religion. In the aftermath of the attacks, the faith was at the center of heated political rhetoric about the threat to women, the threat to the Middle East, the threat to freedom itself that Islam posed. As Arsalan Iftikhar points out in this volume, Islam was framed as some sort of monolith that needed to be knocked down, not as a religion with millions upon millions of practitioners holding diverse views and understandings of their faith.

This is the context in which I found myself that hot, humid August afternoon.

Muslim Voices, the podcast for which I was reporting, was designed to help cut through the totalizing cultural and political framings of Islam. Our goal was to help create spaces where the multifaceted nature of Islam and of Muslim lives would be accessible to the general public. We hoped to counter stereotypes, which is what took me to small-town Indiana. Our plan was to launch the podcast with two pieces exploring stereotypes, one from the perspective of non-Muslims and the other from the perspective of Muslims. The idea was to create an open dialogue about the stereotypes we all hold in order to move past them. *Muslim Voices* was based in a college town, and our advisory board decided it would be best if I went someplace else, someplace more like the rest of America than the liberal community in which we sat.

I'll be honest; I was cursing the advisory board in my head that entire afternoon.

Stereotype Breeds Fear

Here's the thing about stereotyping: it produces fear. Not just fear in the abstract, but fear in the concrete, fear that leads to media personalities admitting that people in "Muslim garb" make them nervous, fear that leads to the firebombing of mosques and the banning of headscarves and burkinis, fear that leads to immigration policy that seems to specifically target individuals from Muslim-majority countries.

Fear, too, seems to be fueling the conversations Americans are having about the place of Islam in the United States. There has been media coverage of terrorist acts carried out in Europe and the United States in the name of the Islamic State, with pundits asking audiences, "Who will be next?" and individuals in social media wondering if their Muslims neighbors are really worth trusting. There are magazine covers claiming to explain why Muslims feel "rage" and to help readers understand just how Islamic the Islamic State is. The 2016 US presidential campaign saw then Republican front-runner Donald Trump make wild accusations about the beliefs of the family of a deceased Gold Star soldier and also suggest that maybe Muslims should not be allowed into the United States. In fact, one of the very first actions President Donald Trump performed upon taking office in January 2017 was to sign an executive order restricting travel into the United States from seven Muslim-majority countries. What has come to be called the "Muslim travel ban" has been knocked down by federal judges, each time spurring politicians and pundits who support the ban to suggest that the United States is less safe if Muslims are allowed to freely travel here.

This coverage comes at the same time that news outlets are filled with stories of communities trying to stop the construction of mosques, as though disallowing the building of a mosque somehow negates the existence of Muslims in America. There has also been an increase over the course of the past year of hate crimes committed against both Muslim and Jewish communities in the United States; it's become such a problem that now news stories are regularly produced detailing how the communities are coming together to counter such hate.

Several years ago, I worked on a research project that explored news media coverage of what was called the Ground Zero Mosque. If you'll recall, a controversy erupted over whether a Muslim community center should be built not far from the site of the September 11th terrorist attacks. News coverage was full of indignant individuals, some who have made a living pushing their Islamophobic and anti-Muslim views, claiming the construction of the community center in a former Burlington Coat Factory building was a type of sacrilege. CNN and other broadcast news outlets featured debates and roundtables on the subject. The community center, if you were wondering, was never built. The research I was part of explored how media coverage of the controversy, and others like it, influenced how individuals felt toward Islam. I'm sure this will come as no surprise, but our research showed a relationship between the coverage and the rise of anti-Muslim sentiment, meaning that if you followed the controversy you were more likely to hold unfavorable views of Islam and Muslims.[2]

Media matters. Words matter. That old adage our parents told us, "Sticks and stones may break my bones but words will never hurt me," is patently untrue. The way journalists choose to cover communities, particularly marginalized communities, plays a big part in shaping how the public views those communities. If Muslims are only ever portrayed as a threat or as people to fear, is it any surprise Islamophobia and anti-Muslim sentiment has been on the rise?

SLAMMED DOORS AND CLOSED MINDS

I like to think I've cultivated an easygoing manner as a journalist, an approachable manner. I generally don't have problems interviewing people once they decide to talk to me. I joke and laugh and make small talk and weave my main questions into our conversations so it feels less like a formal interview than it does a chat with a friendly stranger. My first interview took place in the parking lot of a shopping complex. I saw a young woman loading up her SUV and approached.

"Hi," I said, my recorder, microphone, and headphones in plain view. "I'm Rosemary. I'm talking to people about religion today. Do you have time to answer a few questions?"

The woman looked me up and down, must have decided I posed no threat (or she had Mace handy), and agreed to be interviewed. The conversation went okay. I got a few sound bites I thought I might be able to use, but I was concerned that she mumbled a bit too much during her answers. There was also the issue of how her demeanor had changed once I'd gotten to the questions about Islam. She'd gotten nervous, fidgety. When I said the word "Islam," she'd actually physically jumped the way you might jump from a slight shock or from touching a hot pan. But I felt confident. I had one interview out of the way, I was feeling like maybe the advisory board was right and this was a good idea.

And then came the onslaught of slammed car doors, of being called unChristian, of being actually cursed at. Each time was the same, I'd walk up to someone, introduce myself, start a friendly conversation, and then eventually work my way to questions about Islam or Muslims.

Each time the person I was talking to would shut down immediately. One gentleman actually told me to get out of the way because he'd have no problem hitting me with his car. The young woman in the parking lot wasn't the only person to jump away from me; people physically recoiled from the words "Islam" or "Muslim." I had better luck getting people in an incredibly conservative southern town to talk to me about HIV/AIDS than I did getting people to talk to me about Islam. So much of it seemed fueled by fear, with more than one person that afternoon saying to me as they moved away, "They want to kill us all."

It was, by far, the most difficult reporting day I've ever had. It ended with my standing on a street corner near a courthouse talking for an hour with a man who would not answer any of my questions but who lectured me on the violent history of Islam's conquest of Arabia and how we were next. "There's still time," he told me, "to embrace Christ." We would all die by the sword, the man told me, if we didn't stop the Muslims.

Clearly our idea about starting the podcast with episodes about stereotypes wasn't going to work. Partly because I couldn't get the sound necessary to create them and partly because I was unwilling to use the sound I had gathered. I could have, but it would have turned those people I interviewed into little more than caricatures. It seemed an unproductive way to begin a podcast series, and a project, designed to create safe spaces for dialogue and debate. I went home dejected, but even more committed to the goals of *Muslim Voices*. If that hot, sweaty, miserable Indiana afternoon taught me anything, it was just how very needed real dialogue and real spaces of understanding are.

The question remained: How to create them?

CREATING COMMUNITY CONNECTIONS

I am not a scholar of Islam. I study media and am a former journalist. I knew I had a lot to learn as I began creating the content that would become not one, but two, podcast series. Robert King, in his chapter on reporting on Islam, discusses the importance of working with local Muslim communities. It's great advice—advice anyone covering any kind of beat should take to heart. And it's especially important for individuals covering marginalized communities. When you reach out to those you write about, when you treat them as human beings and not objects, you create opportunities for better, more nuanced reporting. The kind of reporting that earns you respect not only from those you cover, but also from your colleagues.

Voices and Visions of Islam and Muslims from a Global Perspective, the parent of *Muslim Voices*, was a project built on partnerships. Our advisory board was made up of academics from various departments who were all knowledgeable about Islam in a particular perspective. We also reached out to the Islamic Center of Bloomington, Indiana, for insight into ways to bridge the Muslim and non-Muslim communities. We wanted to hear what stories they thought we should be covering, what issues they felt people most misunderstood about Islam. One of the mosque's board members eventually served as the copy editor for our *Crash Course in Islam* podcast, ensuring that the copy was understandable as well as correct. The Bloomington mosque also served as our entry point into the local Muslim community. We attended Eid al-Fitr celebrations, producing a story about the holiday and making contacts that would help shape podcasts in the future. All along the way, the then president of the mosque and many of his board members worked with us to help make sure we were getting what we needed.

The key to creating the types of open spaces for dialogue we aimed for was to work with our local Muslim communities. That wasn't always easy. Even small Muslim communities are diverse, with individuals having their own understandings of their faith and sometimes pushing you to accept that understanding as the most correct one. There were heated conversations about the types of people we should and should not be including in our stories, heated conversations about which voices we should be highlighting in our podcast. And, of course, those conversations could be frustrating. But we were having them. That was the important thing. We had created connections with the scholars and the believers we worked with that allowed us to have sometimes frustrating but always productive conversations. Our project was better for them. It gave us insight into how Muslim audiences might respond to our work, it helped us think through ways to be representative that weren't reductive, and it gave those we worked with an opportunity to really understand where we were coming from. Creating spaces where that kind of dialogue can happen seems to be only growing in importance, not diminishing. Luckily there are now so many more such spaces doing similar things—Qantara in Germany, Patheos's various Muslim blogs, the

Islamic Monthly, Muslimah Media Watch—that it feels like we are inching ever closer to understanding.

The Takeaways

Muslim Voices was a particular type of media product. We were the production of a larger project that was built on partnerships. When I joined the project staff to aid in the production of *Muslim Voices*, relationships with various Indiana University departments and scholars had already been forged. During my work with the project, we extended those relationships to eventually include a local arts foundation, the local mosque, a Muslim student group, and Muslim writers and media personalities working both inside and outside the United States. The podcast was once in iTunes Top 25 podcasts for Islam, and the *Muslim Voices* Twitter account has more than a 111,000 followers. It has been so much more successful than anticipated.

That success I lay at the feet of our willingness to talk, our willingness to be open, and a continual revaluation of our goals and aims. *Muslim Voices* was not a straight news production. It was designed to be both educational and informational. The overarching goal was to help dispel myths and stereotypes associated with Islam and Muslims. So, perhaps, our task was a bit easier than that of a general assignment reporter doing a story on a local Muslim community. But I do think there are some takeaways from our project that can help news reporters better serve their communities and be able to move away from narratives about Islam and Muslims that trap them in stereotype.

Lessons for Reporters

Adopt a Muslim (or several)—During a science reporting fellowship, a speaker suggested we all adopt a scientist, someone we trusted to help us decide what stories were worth reporting and what science might be junk. I think this can be useful for reporters working in any beat, but when you are covering a marginalized group, having someone you trust to run story ideas by is invaluable. I was lucky my job gave me access to members of the local mosque's board, but I also made friends with several Muslims from different backgrounds. I'd run ideas by them to figure out what might be worth pursuing and what might be bunk. They were also the people I asked questions that I might not be comfortable asking anyone else because I knew I could trust them. No one wants to look stupid when in the field; having people I knew I could turn to for information made me more comfortable, and confident, with the job I was doing.

Get a good translation of the Qur'an—This does not mean you have to read it cover to cover, but becoming familiar with the text can be helpful when you are covering stories about Muslim communities. There are a lot of accusations about what the Qur'an sanctions. Instead of taking those verbatim, open a Qur'an and see what it says before running out to write about how Islam condones wife beating or the slaying of infidels or whatever other inflammatory thing is being said. Good reporters do their research. Having a Qur'an handy can help you do that when covering stories about Muslims.

Visit the local mosque—During Ramadan many mosques will hold iftars, evening meals to break the day's fast, for the entire community. Find out if mosques where you are hold these types of public, interfaith, iftars and show up to one. If the local Muslim community holds a big Eid-al-Fitr celebration that is open to the public, put some face time in, even if you don't cover the holiday for your news outlet. We are taught to cultivate sources. Without good sources, we can't do our job. Look to the local Muslim community as a source for stories, not just a thing to be reported on.

Follow Muslims in social media—There are a lot of really interesting things happening in Twitter. Conversations about various aspects of Islam are taking place under different hashtags several times a month. Muslims from all over the world, and from all traditions, use the space to discuss politics, their identity, and their faith. There may even be Muslims in your local community using Twitter, or other social media, to write about their lives. Find these individuals. Follow them. Interact with them. Social media can be a great tool for finding sources, but also for learning more about whatever beat you are covering. You might even find some story ideas you hadn't considered. Our *Muslim Voices* Twitter account took off in a way we never expected and has yielded relationships and stories I would not have been able to access otherwise.

Those are my four pieces of practical advice for reporters who will be covering stories about Islam or Muslim communities. It's all rather straightforward. It takes some time and effort, but in the end all good reporting does. Reporters are trained as generalists. No one expects you to be an expert in everything you cover. That would be impossible. But you do need to be curious. If you aren't curious about life and people and stories then you are in the wrong profession. That curiosity should drive you to learn more about whatever it is you are covering, be it a medical story, a political story, or one about Islam. Taking that time to learn more, taking that time to do your research, will make you a better reporter. It will also help you cut through spin and get to the heart of a story.

The thing to remember is that there's never going to be enough time. You're never going to have enough time to tell the perfect story. You're never going to be able to include all perspectives on an issue. It's impossible. What is possible, however, is being thoughtful. What is possible is understanding enough background so that when you decide what voices and perspectives to include in your stories you can feel confident with those choices. What is possible is producing, through a number of different stories, a nuanced and complex picture of what you are reporting on, of whom you are reporting on.

The work we do as journalists has real heft, real weight. Reporting done well has the potential to bring injustice to light, to hold the powerful accountable for their behavior, to provide space for the marginalized to speak. Those are the reasons I became a reporter in the first place; I felt a calling to make the world a better place, and journalism seemed like one way I could do that. But just as journalism can make things better, it can also make things worse. It can feed fuel to political conversations full of hate and fear, it can perpetuate misunderstandings and harmful myths, and it can harden the boundaries we put up between "Us" and "Them." Uncritical reporting leads to afternoons full of people running at the mere mention of Muslims. We have to do better. If we really believe ourselves to be an integral part of the social fabric of where we live, we have to do a better job representing all the people who live in our communities, not just those with whom we are most familiar.

Rosemary Pennington is Assistant Professor of Journalism at Miami University. Since 2008 she has been involved with Indiana University's Voices and Visions project, serving as project coordinator, podcast producer, and managing editor.

TWO

SHATTERING THE MUSLIM MONOLITH

Arsalan Iftikhar

As a prominent American Muslim global media commentator since the September 11 attacks, one of the many things that keeps me awake at night is our Western media's inability to view Islam and Muslims as anything more than a static monolithic entity. From perpetuating the societal falsehood that "all Arabs are Muslims and all Muslims are Arabs" to the catch-all term "terrorism" being co-opted to only apply to acts perpetrated by Muslims, American journalists can learn many lessons by choosing to shatter this "Muslim monolith" paradigm in their daily coverage of news events. From the use of tired stereotypical black burka stock photos for any story dealing with Muslim women's issues to understanding the ethnic demographic diversity of the entire American Muslim community, journalists from print, radio, and television broadcast mediums can help enrich their coverage of Islam and Muslims by delving a bit deeper to create more nuanced coverage of Islam and Muslims.

WHO ARE MUSLIMS?

The first major monolithic narrative that requires societal redress is the "All Arabs are Muslims" and "All Muslims are Arabs" false metanarrative that has seeped into much of American society today. In order to understand the diversity of the global Muslim community, we must understand global demographic trends. According to an April 2015 study published by the Pew Forum on Religion and Life,[1] Islam is the fastest-growing religion in the world. The world's Muslim population is expected to increase by about 73 percent over a forty-year period, rising from 1.6 billion in 2010 to 2.76 billion by 2050. This rapid growth means the global Muslim and Christian populations will be virtually the same by 2050. Of particular interest given recent debates over the flow of refugees and immigrants into the United States and western Europe, Pew projects that by 2050 the population of North America will be 2.4 percent Muslim while the population of Europe will be 10.2 percent Muslim. That same Pew study also identified the ten countries with the largest Muslim populations. The top five—Indonesia, India, Pakistan, Bangladesh, and Nigeria—all sit outside the Middle East or North Africa, the region popularly associated with Islam.

Generally speaking, according to the Arab Anti-Discrimination Committee (ADC), the term "Arabs" usually refers to people who speak Arabic as their first language.[2] According to the BBC, Arabic is the native language of more than two hundred million people worldwide.[3] Estimates show that the "Arab world" consists of twenty-two countries in the Middle East and North Africa where Arabic is the principal (although not the only) language spoken. Arabs are united by language, culture, and history, but they are religiously diverse: most Arabs are Muslims, but there are also millions of Christian Arabs and thousands of Jewish Arabs as well. People from Arab-majority nations have come to the United States in several major waves, beginning in the late nineteenth century.[4] Although they share a common linguistic and cultural heritage, Arab Americans are a highly diverse and nonmonolithic group as well.

According to the Arab American Institute (AAI), while all twenty-two Arab countries have sent emigrants to the United States, "the majority of Arab Americans have ancestral ties to Lebanon, Syria, Palestine, Egypt and Iraq."[5] Most Americans are also totally unaware that a majority of Arab Americans are Christians (Catholic, Orthodox, and Protestant), as many of them descended from the first major wave that consisted mainly of Syrian and Lebanese Christian merchants. A second wave of Arab immigration that started after World War II, however, is overwhelmingly Muslim, making Muslims the fastest-growing segment of the Arab American community today.

The vast majority of the American Muslim community, however, is not Arab, so it is important to get a lay of the demographic land for the rest of the

American community. A 2009 Gallup poll suggests the American Muslim population is "the most racially diverse group"[6] the organization has surveyed in the United States. What might surprise some is that 35 percent of Muslim Americans are black, making that the largest racial subgroup within the Muslim American population. Muslims in the United States who have descended from immigrants also come from diverse backgrounds, with Pew noting that although more Muslim Americans can point to the Middle East or North Africa as their family's place of origin than any other region, the country that has sent the most Muslim emigrants to the United States is actually Pakistan.[7]

Within the past ten years, there can be little debate that the one religion covered most by the media has been Islam. According to a February 2012 report from the Pew Research Center's Project for Excellence in Journalism,[8] of all the major religions covered by the American mainstream media, there was no religion that was the subject of more stories (31.3 percent of total religion stories) than Islam (with Protestantism a distant second with 20 percent of stories). The same report found that "six of the top 10 religion stories of 2011 were about Islam. This continues a trend first seen in 2010, when four of the top five religion stories [of the year] involved controversies related to Islam."

In the year 2011 alone, we saw major national controversies erupt in the news. In addition to a nutty, Qur'an-burning, mustached pastor in Florida and the right-wing national uproar over the "Ground Zero Mosque," we saw prominent politicians capitalizing on these negative Muslim narratives to score cheap political points, solidify their conservative political base, and activate xenophobic nativist fears under the banner of fighting against the euphemism of "political correctness."

A high-profile media circus perpetuating the "only Muslims can be terrorists" monolithic narrative occurred in March 2011. Congressman Peter King (R-NY) provided a new form of political legitimacy for this anti-Muslim societal bias when he decided to hold a congressional hearing on "The Extent of Radicalization in the American Muslim Community and that Community's Response." Reminiscent of the shadow cast by the McCarthy era, these congressional hearings signaled that Congress thought it was now acceptable to investigate protected First Amendment religious beliefs, practices, and activities of American Muslims simply because of their faith.

"Rep. King's intent seems clear: To cast suspicion upon all Muslim Americans and to stoke the fires of anti-Muslim prejudice and Islamophobia," wrote Congressman Michael Honda (D-CA) in a February 2011 opinion editorial for the *San Francisco Chronicle*.[9] Calling the congressional hearings a "sinister" ploy by King, Honda continued: "By framing his hearings as an investigation of the American Muslim community, the implication is that we should be suspicious of our Muslim neighbors, co-workers or classmates solely on the basis of their religion. This should be deeply troubling to Americans of all races and religions. An investigation specifically targeting a single religion implies, erroneously, a dangerous disloyalty, with one broad sweep of the discriminatory brush."

Similarly, national security experts like Richard Clarke—who was well-known as counterterrorism "czar" to both presidents Bill Clinton and George W. Bush—told the *Los Angeles Times*, "To the extent that these hearings make American Muslims feel that they are the object of fear-mongering, it will only serve Al Qaeda's ends."[10]

The advent of what's been labeled the Islamic State has made this an even more pressing issue. The terrorist group has taken over control of large swaths of Iraq and Syria and has inspired attacks in Europe and the United States.[11] The barbarity of ISIS's actions gained the group attention, as did the way ISIS manipulated the news media into covering its actions the way it wanted to be covered. An *Atlantic* article[12] about the 2016 attack on Brussels noted, "In the avalanche of uncertainty that followed the attacks, the ISIS propagandists were able to dictate their story—literally word for word—to an international, and specifically Western, audience. Releasing the claim of responsibility first in English was no mistake. Directed, first and foremost, at the Western enemies of ISIS, the statement was a way to capitalize on the international media storm surrounding Brussels that day. Be it through headlines or tweets, the propagandists manipulated a global audience, opponents and sympathizers alike, to disseminate their message of intimidation and enhance the perception of ISIS's threat."

Additionally, the group has been adept at using social media to disseminate its message itself, often targeting young Muslims who feel alienated or marginalized in the countries where they live and recruiting them to travel to Iraq or Syria and support ISIS's work.[13]

Muslim Women's Issues

Another troubling monolithic narrative found in Western media outlets is the coverage of Muslim women's issues and how this coverage only perpetuates certain negative tropes that people have about Islam today. If you ask many American Muslims, they will say that whenever they see stories about Muslim women, the vast majority of these stories revolve around sensationalist issues like the hijab (headscarf), female genital mutilation (FGM), honor killings, or burka bans in European nations. News coverage in the summer of 2016 provided a clear example of this as reporters covered the debate over the attempt to ban the burkini—a wetsuit-like garment designed for devout Muslim women to wear at the beach—in a small French town near Nice, France. One photo of police enforcing the ban was seared on the minds of many as it showed officers standing over a Muslim woman as she was forced to take off her burkini while sitting in public on a beach.[14]

As writer Fatemeh Fakhraie once noted, "News stories about [Muslim women] are fixated on appearance. Most major stories about Muslim women revolve around how they look and what they're wearing—not who they are and what they are doing. . . . This isn't much different from coverage in years past, and it doesn't mean that their media images are any more accurate or well-rounded."[15] Such coverage perpetuates Orientalist and at times Islamophobic understandings of the lives of Muslim women, as Rafia Zakaria discusses in this book.

According to *InterCultures* magazine in Canada, there are many reasons for such "essentialist" representations of women in Islamic cultures. Journalistic constraints such as "deadline pressures, length requirements and reader accessibility" force stories to be brief and underinvestigated, which leads to stories that can perpetuate stereotypes against Muslim women. Dr. Karim H. Karim, director of the School of Journalism and Communication at Carleton University, suggests that "because the editor at home will not have a good understanding of what is happening on the ground, which the foreign correspondent does, they will reinstate the dominant discourses of the stereotypes the correspondent is trying to fight against. Even within the newsroom there are struggles going on in terms of representation: a picture may be added to an article which completely subverts the intention of the writer."[16]

An interesting examination of the Western media's coverage of Muslim women was conducted by British freelance journalist Arwa Aburawa. In September 2010, Aburawa wrote about her analysis of ten years' worth of the British-edition of *Marie Claire* magazine (minus thirty-five issues that were missing from the archives) to measure the number of times Muslim women were covered in *Marie Claire* magazine.[17] Her research found that "Muslim women were covered in around 44 percent of all the magazines I searched: roughly, one article per magazine was deemed as representation in that issue. Most of that coverage was on Muslim women from developing countries such as Afghanistan (a whopping 11 articles) rather than those from Britain (only 4 articles), but overall Muslim women were well-represented." From her qualitative analysis, she found that "exactly half [of the magazine articles] portrayed Muslim women as victims, while the other half showed them as independent, empowered women. This may seem like a mixed outcome, but the fact that half of the articles showed Muslim women as non-victims is a pretty unexpected result. What's more, the veil was barely mentioned in articles as oppressive (the only two cases were in Afghanistan, so they may even be justified) and Islam was rarely mentioned as imposed or oppressive."

She concluded by saying, "I don't want to say that the notion that Muslim women are stereotyped as powerless victims oppressed is false, but just maybe it's more complicated. Looking back, there were some really awful articles, like 'My husband was a suicide bomber' or 'Sold into marriage at 11,' which definitely painted Muslim women as victims. But there were also some really great articles, such as 'I am Muslim and British' and one that covered the biggest matriarchal society in the world (which happens to be in the heart of Muslim Indonesia)."

Negative Portrayal; Negative Perceptions

With such staggering monolithic negative narratives about Islam and Muslims pervasive in our Western media today, it should also come as no surprise that this reductive societal marginalization has produced negative feelings in the general public toward Muslims. Research conducted at Indiana University in 2012–2013 found a relationship between negative news media coverage of Islam and Muslims and a rise in anti-Muslim sentiment in the United States and Europe.[18] In a 2011 study of the way Muslims and non-Muslims viewed one another, Pew found that non-Muslims were most likely to view Muslims as fanatical, violent, arrogant, and selfish.[19] This research is in line with earlier surveys and studies that identified an overall negative feeling toward Islam among the American people.

A December 2004 public opinion poll commissioned by Cornell University[20] found that about 44 percent of Americans said they believe that "some curtailment of civil liberties is necessary for Muslim-Americans." Similarly, more than 26 percent of Americans in the same poll stated that they believe that American mosques should be closely monitored by US law enforcement agencies and more than 29 percent of Americans agreed that undercover law enforcement agents should infiltrate Muslim civic and volunteer organizations in order to keep tabs on their activities and fundraising. Nearly the same overall public sentiments were captured in a March 2006 *Washington Post* / ABC News poll,[21] which found that more than 46 percent of Americans said that they personally held "unfavorable views" about Islam and Muslims. In that same public opinion poll, about one-fourth of the respondents admitted to feelings of prejudice: 27 percent said that they held "prejudiced feelings" toward Muslims, whereas 25 percent of Americans polled said that they have prejudiced feelings against Arabs.

The sheer (and mind-boggling) hysteria of post-9/11 America came to light when a July 2005 *USA TODAY* / CNN / Gallup poll[22] found that nearly 53 percent of Americans were in favor of "requiring all Arabs, including those who are U.S. citizens, to undergo special, more intensive security checks before boarding airplanes." In the same July 2005 poll, the most shocking finding was that more than 46 percent of Americans favored "requiring Arabs [and Muslims], including those who are US citizens, to carry a special ID" during their daily lives. There is some hope that attitudes may be changing. And, ironically, some suggest that President Donald Trump might be a cause of this shift.

During the 2016 presidential campaign, several public opinion polls actually showed an increase in Americans' favorable ratings of Muslims. As Shibley Telhami, writing for the *Washington Post's Monkey Cage* blog, notes,

"This kind of large shift does not normally take place in one year unless there are extraordinary events taking place."[23] Telhami goes on to suggest that part of the reason for that shift is a jump in the way specifically Democrats viewed Islam and Muslims: "Among Democrats, the shift was significant enough to impact overall results. Favorable attitudes toward Muslims improved from 67 percent to 81 percent. Favorable attitudes toward Islam went from 51 percent to 66 percent."

Telhami writes that then GOP candidate Donald Trump's harsh rhetoric about Muslims—suggesting they were dangerous threats to American lives and that Islam was inherently violent—put Democratic politicians in a position to push a counternarrative that worked to frame Muslims as American and Islam as no more violent than any other religion. The result may have been to create more favorable feelings toward Muslims and Islam among Democrats and independents. This partisan shift in Americans' views on Islam also showed up in data from the Brookings Institution. In a two-part survey of American attitudes toward the faith and its believers conducted before and after the Orlando shootings, the organization found that 79 percent of Democrats held a favorable view of Muslims while only 49 percent of Republicans did.[24] At the same time, a mid-February 2017 poll by Pew found that Americans still have the coolest feelings toward Islam.[25] So while attitudes may be changing, it's slow going.

Although there is not one fell journalistic swoop that will help Americans understand the diversity and nuance of the American Muslim community, one of the best ways to move the discussion in the right direction would be for American journalists to educate their audiences and help shatter some of the aforementioned monolithic metanarratives that have bogged down journalistic portrayals of Muslims for far too long. And there do seem to be projects being developed to do that. The Society of Professional Journalists launched in 2017 its "Muslimedia" program. Muslimedia provides resources for journalists and Muslim communities to stage public discussions in mosques focused on the news media's portrayal of Islam and Muslim life.[26] If news coverage of Muslims is to improve, more open and honest conversations like the ones the Society of Professional Journalists is attempting to facilitate must take place. Otherwise the cycle of stereotyped coverage will continue.

Arsalan Iftikhar is an author, international human rights lawyer, founder of TheMuslimGuy.com, and senior editor of the *Islamic Monthly* magazine. He is author of *Scapegoats: How Islamophobia Helps Our Enemies and Threatens Our Freedoms.*

THREE

SO NEAR, YET SO FAR: AN ACADEMIC REFLECTION ON THE ENDURANCE OF AMERICAN ISLAMOPHOBIA

Peter Gottschalk

IN MARCH 2011, TERRY JONES burned a copy of the Qur'an. When he had threatened to do so nearly a year earlier, he made headlines and newscasts, which earned him a call from the commander of US forces in Afghanistan, Gen. David Petraeus, imploring him to desist. Yet when he finally moved beyond threats to action, few news outlets reported the event. Ultimately, Jones's exhibition garnered only 3.7 percent of mainstream news sources' religion coverage for the year, in comparison to his 2010 threats, which gained 14.5 percent of coverage for the year.[1] Although the fact that this pastor for a fifty-congregant church attracted a twenty-fifth of all the national news reporting on religion is not insignificant, the change seemed a victory for those who had protested the skewed portrayal of Muslims and Islamic traditions among American news outlets. It suggested that editors had rethought how they were amplifying the message of an Islamophobic provocateur, publicly unknown otherwise. Unfortunately, when some Afghans—outraged at the revelation regarding Jones's "trial" and "execution" of the Qur'an—rioted and killed United Nations workers, their violence made the story topical again, and so editors put aside their earlier inhibitions and reported the deaths and Jones's provocations that helped spark them.

This unhappy event demonstrates how journalistic efforts to avoid the reaffirmation of Islamophobic and anti-Muslim sentiments have attained limited success. Since the September 11 attacks, many Americans have willingly endured a learning curve in their efforts to respond intelligently and empathetically to all those impacted by the events. Hollywood filmmakers, law enforcement, scholars, newscasters, editors, mosques, churches, synagogues, Muslims, Christians, Jews, and atheists have all struggled to make sense of both the tragedies and the lingering sense of threat from violent organizations like al-Qaeda. Some Americans have re-embraced preexisting paradigms while others—sensing the limitations of these earlier explanations and responses—have sought new approaches to future understanding and action. Many journalists have been at the forefront of these constructive efforts, as reflected in the shifts evident in reporting about Muslims, Islamic traditions, and the country's domestic and international tensions. Nevertheless, as the Jones event demonstrates, even the most informed journalist remains captive—if only because of demands from editors and expectations of audiences—both to the centuries-old stereotypes about Muslims and their religion and to the dynamics of Islamophobia in twenty-first-century America.

Based on my experience as an educator serving in both university and public settings, I have concluded that journalists might benefit from nine ideas scholars of religion have developed when engaging American views of Muslims and Islamic cultures. It is important to note that many of the issues described here might pertain to any religion that an American would attempt to understand as an outsider.

ISLAMOPHOBIC AND ANTI-MUSLIM SENTIMENT ARE AS OLD AS RACISM IN THE UNITED STATES

Western suspicion of Muslims and Islamic traditions does not date back to just 2001, or to the Iranian Revolution of 1979, or even to the battle against the Barbary pirates in the early nineteenth century, America's first war abroad. Such fears were endemic among the Europeans who traded and settled in and outside the Spanish, French, and British colonies of North America. Long before these merchants, missionaries, and settlers organized to cross the Atlantic, the medieval western European church had inculcated an abiding concern about Muslims. "Christendom," as the Roman Church termed the realms under Christian dominion, had suffered major setbacks in the first century following Muhammad's death (632 CE). The east coast of the Mediterranean, North Africa, and the Iberian Peninsula had represented some of the oldest and most thoroughly Christian lands. Yet by the middle of the eighth century, not only had these lands come under Muslim rule, but a great proportion of their Christian populations had converted voluntarily to Islam.

In light of these unexpected setbacks, various medieval Christian writers viewed Muhammad as a heretic at best and the Antichrist at worst. Muslims, therefore, were either blaspheming Christians or minions of Satan. As Mediterranean Muslim power waned at the beginning of the modern era, European Christian power ascended, as the dispatch of ships of exploration, then expeditions of plunder, and finally endeavors of colonization demonstrated. During this period, Europeans became fascinated with what they considered the corrupted opulence and cruel control of "Oriental despots" and the oppressive treatment of Muslim women by men, interests informed in no small way by an increasing European self-confidence and sense of superiority. A seventeenth-century volume on the life of Muhammad ascribed to Sir Walter Raleigh, founder of America's first English colony, claimed "the Devill, taking advantage upon his weaknes [sic], enflamed his heart with pride, which wrought in him a desire to be esteemed a Prophet, thinking all other attributes of Religion and sanctity to be but vile and base."[2] Despite the declining political power of Muslims just before and during European expansionism, among Christian Europeans, Muslim fighting men retained a reputation for formidableness common since the Crusades. Meanwhile, in general Muslims more successfully resisted Christian proselytization than most other groups. And so Orientalist writers and artists—who asserted an authoritative understanding of these people—commonly described Muslim men as zealous, narrow-minded, and combative, while Muslim women were their subjugated (albeit titillating) victims. Despite the age of these seeds of prejudice, their prevalence in American soil has meant that Islamophobia and anti-Muslim attitudes have cropped up repeatedly throughout US history. Each new season, however, has taken its particular shape according to the specific political conditions and general cultural concerns of the day.

Islamophobic and Anti-Muslim Sentiments Are Significantly Different, But Not Distinct

While neologisms are approached with appropriate suspicion, differences in prejudice justify these two specific terms. "Islamophobia" refers to an unjustified social anxiety regarding Islamic traditions. When Jones burned the Qur'an, he expressed exactly this fear, destroying a text he judged central to those traditions and, hence, central to the danger posed to Christians, if not to humanity. In contrast, the stereotyped image of Muslims as dangerous (if male) and oppressed (if female) Middle Easterners often (though decreasingly) seen in Hollywood films expresses an anti-Muslim stereotype. While Muslims may be dangerous or oppressed because of "Islam," they are identifiable because of a racial stereotype. In fact, only 20 percent of the world's Muslims have a Middle Eastern heritage, a fact that surprises many Americans because of the focus of media attention on that region and the pervasiveness of the stereotype. Hence, distinguishing the source of anxiety that motivates antagonism—a simplified portrait of a multifaceted set of religious traditions or a stereotyped caricature of a multiracial collection of religious adherents—provides detail and insight.

Anything Seen from Afar Looks Singular and Undifferentiated

Half of Americans have no direct contact with Muslims, or so they think. A 2016 Pew Center poll found that 47 percent of respondents did not know anyone who was Muslim.[3] Meanwhile, a Reuters poll a year earlier found that 68 percent of respondents replied that Islam posed a threat to the United States.[4] These negative indicators have increased *since 9/11*.[5] It would appear likely that among other costs, the decade of combat against al-Qaeda, Afghan Taliban, Iraqi insurgents, and the so-called "Islamic State"—coupled with domestic violence associated with these and similar groups—have reinforced the centuries-old view of Muslims as inherently violent. Even though Muslim Afghans and Iraqis have fought and died alongside US troops and that the majority of Muslim leaders and laypeople have decried religious violence, news sources have tended to highlight violence against Americans and other Westerners with little attention to the Muslims included within these groups. Even the loss in combat of American Muslim troops has gone largely overlooked by non-Muslim Americans whose focus is on the distant Islamic traditions of foreign Muslims. Presidential candidate Donald Trump's 2016 mockery of the parents of a Muslim serviceman killed in combat provided a rare moment of media and popular attention to Muslim American sacrifices.

WHEN SOMEONE WHO HAPPENS TO BE MUSLIM DOES SOMETHING NEWSWORTHY, SHE OR HE TENDS TO BE IDENTIFIED AS A MUSLIM IN THE EYES OF MOST AMERICANS

But when someone who happens to be Christian acts comparably, they tend not to be so identified. American journalism has addressed similar biases during the course of its history. For instance, journalists accepted the challenge brought by people of color who protested news coverage that only identified nonwhites by their race. Similar changes ensued when feminists pointed out the normative place of men in reporting. In the past decade, news outlets have made efforts in this vein in regard to their description of Muslims.

Nevertheless, the expectation that anyone who happens to be Muslim must be primarily defined by her religion remains among many Christian Americans. For them, countries with a majority of Muslims, such as Pakistan or Morocco, are "Islamic nations." Such labels suggest that religion serves as the primary characteristic of the nation and its people. Conversely, Americans seldom identify North American and European countries as "Christian nations," despite their Christian majorities. Part of this dynamic stems from a Christian norm in the United States that assumes Americans are Christian unless identified otherwise, and part of it stems from secular ideals that avoid describing the country in religious terms. Certainly many evangelical and fundamentalist Christians assert that the country's founders intended to create a Christian nation, but such claims make many other Americans uncomfortable. Whether originating from a Christian or secular norm, the unwillingness to describe Western countries as inherently religious makes countries that *are* described in this manner appear inherently and definitively religious. In fact, most Muslim-majority countries demonstrate a vast diversity of sentiments among their populations about how much they wish to involve Islamic traditions in their family lives, politics, economics, and judiciary. Regardless, while "Christendom" has largely disappeared as a concept, one hears repeated mention by journalists, scholars, and others of "the Islamic world" or "the Muslim world," as though this is a self-contained and uniformly Muslim place quite distinct from other societies.

AMERICANS KNOW LITTLE ABOUT RELIGIONS OTHER THAN THEIR OWN (IF THEY HAVE ONE)

Despite the laudable, decade-long effort by places of worship, Islamic organizations, news outlets, educational institutions, and public broadcasting to educate Americans about Muslims and Islamic traditions, 55 percent of Americans in 2011 reported that they do not have a basic understanding of "Islam."[6] While this represents a gradual decline from the 65 percent who reported the same in 2002, it reflects a larger condition of US society. Most American children attend public schools, and many, if not most, of those schools avoid teaching anything about religions out of concern for maintaining the church-state separation. The inherent antipathies inherited from the larger culture, therefore, find little counterbalance from education. Moreover, popular culture offers few insights: although 77 percent of Americans said that religion was "very" or "somewhat" important to them,[7] television and film show few depictions of Americans acting religiously, although examples have recently increased.[8] Not only does this curtail an important avenue of information for audiences, but it also reinforces the attitudes about Muslims seeming to be unusually religious because they are defined as religious in a medium that portrays nonreligiousness as normative.

Meanwhile, what non-Muslim Americans learn about Muslims from their own religious communities may be implacably hostile. For many conservative Christians, Islamic commitments represent an obstinate obstacle to their evangelical efforts, while many Jewish and Christian supporters of Israel consider Arab antagonism to Zionism as indicative of anti-Jewish sentiments among all Muslims. Hindu nationalist organizations widely disseminate materials about Hindu traditions to Hindu Americans, some of which portray Muslims as India's despoilers. Hence, even those Americans who do know something about Muslims and Islamic traditions do not tend to put that knowledge into a larger, comparative framework that would help mitigate the negative stereotypes about the Muslim forms of religion and culture.

AMERICANS OFTEN ASSUME RELIGIONS TO BE
REDUCIBLE TO A SINGLE SET OF CORE BELIEFS,
PRACTICES, AND AUTHORITATIVE VOICE

If they belong to a religious community, Americans likely recognize the diversity in their larger tradition. Most Catholics tend to understand that not all Christian services run like theirs, and Conservative Jews probably do not expect all Jews to conform to their views. But because of the lack of the more expansive comparative approach mentioned above, Americans commonly view others' religions as fitting a monolithic template: each is adjudicated by a single authority, is based on a single holy book, and is made up of specific beliefs and practices. In other words, Americans tend to hold other people to the beliefs and books that they *suppose* to be central to their religions.

In the case of Muslims, the assumption is that "Islam" uniformly requires Muslims to maintain certain convictions and perform particular actions. In its more egregious forms, this leads to claims such as "Islam requires Muslims to kill infidels." But the seemingly more innocuous idea that "the Qur'an requires women to be subservient to men" is hardly more accurate. For most Muslims, as for members of most other religions, the Qur'an represents only one, albeit very influential, source for understanding. Family traditions, community teachings, cultural variations, and individual interpretations all play crucial roles in how Muslims live their lives. Less informed perspectives treat the Qur'an and "Islam" more broadly as authorities so singular that they appear almost personified. In fact, neither the Qur'an nor any Islamic tradition speaks for itself; each must be interpreted.

Because interpretations of texts and traditions occur in the minds of people, they inherently reflect individual, community, and cultural diversity. When we examine how Jews and Christians engage their bibles—and other religious communities their religious texts if they have any—we notice how some passages may gain great prominence while others fall into obscurity. Holding a group accountable for believing everything written in their important texts misses the point of how the texts remain important in a community's life. Additionally, listening to what specific groups espouse and watching their customs proves much more informative than holding them to some universalized abstraction of their tradition.

Hence, if we replace "Muslims" for "Islam" in each reference to what "Islam believes" or "Islam practices," then we would necessarily be forced to deal with the multiplicity and diversity inherent in any population exceeding a billion people. The Bush and Obama administrations took a parallel step when they eschewed reference to "radical Islam," a term that initially found widespread use. Instead, they emphasized the specific groups, such as al-Qaeda or the so-called "Islamic State," recognizing that despite the adjectival qualifier, the reference to "Islam" inherently connected violent organizations to the religious traditions of all Muslims, if not in the minds of non-Muslim Americans, then certainly in those of Muslims in the United States and beyond.[9] Taking this another step, perhaps both secular scholars and journalists would do well to eliminate altogether their references to "Islam" except when reporting how Muslims use the term. Given that Muslim meanings for this term are myriad and often contradictory, how would non-Muslim authors establish a definitive meaning for their audiences? Yet academic books frequently feature "Islam" in their titles and media reports persistently discuss it. Readers will have noticed that this chapter mentions "Islamic traditions," recognizing that Muslims use the singular term "Islam" as a critically important point of reference, yet often point to it from vastly different directions, social positions, and cultural backgrounds.

Few Members of Religious Communities Believe or Follow Everything Their Leaders Say Is Required

Even when Americans understand the multiplicity within Islamic traditions, they often assume that if an imam, mullah, or other religious leader makes a pronouncement, all Muslims must follow it, or at least pay attention to it. Perhaps the most famous, or infamous, example of this would be the Ayatollah Khomeini's *fatwa* demanding that any Muslim who could should assassinate author Salman Rushdie because of his supposedly blasphemous novel *The Satanic Verses*. No universally accepted Islamic authority exists, and the proclamations of those who are recognized as authoritative are almost always considered debatable. Even the most authoritative Sunni institution, Al-Azhar University in Cairo, hardly speaks with one voice, since it trains Islamic scholars to make independent, individual conclusions. Hence, despite his dramatic gesture, Khomeini could not have expected many Muslims to abide by his 1989 *fatwa* (which literally means "legal opinion"), especially since it represented the individual view of a jurist from the Shia tradition, a minority perspective at best. Two decades later, many Americans portray this event as evidence of Islam's opposition to freedom of expression, anthropomorphizing Islam through the person of Khomeini.

All this notwithstanding, various imams, muftis, mullahs, and other leaders do make pronouncements that influence particular Muslim communities. In most instances, however, their decisions hardly amount to law. To suggest otherwise would be to ascribe far more power to them than they actually enjoy. Very few Muslim traditions have a figure as central as the Vatican or the pope. But then few American Catholics follow the dictates of the Vatican as sanctimoniously as non-Catholics often assume. A 2012 CNN poll found that 88 percent of Catholic respondents believed that Catholics should make up their own minds in regard to moral issues such as abortion and birth control.[10] While many Americans may implicitly understand this freedom of interpretation for their own religion, they often assume the authoritativeness of leaders in other religions.

A Cycle of "Experts," Media, and Political Interests Perpetuate Islamophobia

A report by the Center for American Progress (CAP) and *The Islamophobia Industry* by Nathan Lean have helpfully connected the dots in regard to a pernicious dynamic that has developed in the past decade. The authors demonstrate how a handful of self-appointed experts on Islam such as Daniel Pipes, Pam Geller, Robert Spencer, and David Yerushalmi positioned themselves after 2001 as sources to whom media outlets referred for both extended commentary and sound bites. At times, these figures have served to bring "balance" to a debate regarding Muslims, despite a lack of any credentials except their perseverance to gain a media profile. Beyond this media coverage, organizations established by these professional Islamophobes—such as Middle East Forum and the Stop Islamization of America—have helped legitimate their views in the eyes of the public. Furthermore, the CAP report demonstrates how politically conservative groups such as the Donors Capital Fund and Richard Mellon Scaife foundations have supported these professional "experts" and their organizations.[11] The more news coverage these Islamophobes receive, the more authoritative they appear and the better their publications sell, further elevating their public profile. Fortunately, both news outlets and government branches have since recognized the pernicious and ill-informed nature of these individuals' views and turned elsewhere for sources. Nevertheless, these professional Islamophobes energetically pursue audiences through publications and social media.

Meanwhile, politicians and political candidates often assimilate and repeat Islamophobic views locally, regionally, and nationally. For instance, many of the twenty-three states that have legislation pending or laws to ban the use of sharia law in their courthouses (some under the guise of prohibiting "foreign laws") have borrowed language directly from Yerushalmi's initiatives, such as American Laws for American Courts. Meanwhile, in the 2008 and 2012 presidential elections, various candidates attempted to capitalize on Islamophobic fears by either using Barack Obama's Muslim heritage to cast suspicion on his Christian identity or rallying voters to resist a proposal to build a mosque three blocks from New York's Ground Zero site.[12] Some Republicans, such as Michele Bachmann, Renee Elmers, and Peter King, have proven particularly strident in this regard. Beyond the light of the campaign, King supervised congressional hearings on the radicalization of American Muslims. While half of Americans polled approved of hearings on extremism, a majority disagreed that hearings should focus on Muslims alone.[13] Nevertheless, King pursued and publicized the hearings to national media attention (although various news outlets such as CNN and the *New York Times* offered repeated, negative coverage).

The 2016 presidential campaign offered even higher levels of vitriol. Herman Cain alleged "shariazation" of government, Ben Carson declared that no true Muslim should serve as president, Ted Cruz called on US law enforcement to "patrol and secure Muslim neighborhoods before they become radicalized," Bobby Jindal falsely asserted that Muslims had established exclusive "no-go zones" in some European neighborhoods, Rand Paul argued that building a mosque near Ground Zero was equivalent to a Ku Klux Klan march, and Marco Rubio denied discrimination against Muslims in the United States. The Republican nominee, Donald Trump, made Islamophobic and anti-Muslim claims one of the cornerstones of his campaign, accurately gauging the resonance for these among a small, yet energized, fraction of voters. Parallel with this increased vilification, news media underlined the contributing stereotypes and false claims.

Entertainment Outlets Do Not Tend to Depict Religion, Which Means That the Only Forms of Religion That Find Their Way into Headlines Are "Aberrant" Forms

In many, though not all, parts of the United States, secularism means more than legal protections that keep government separated from religion, and vice versa. It also implies an implicit agreement—more like an ingrained sensibility—that religious people should keep their beliefs and practices to themselves in the privacy of their homes and places of worship. Hence the nervousness many Americans show when inoffensive Mormons and Jehovah's Witnesses come to their door to discuss their beliefs. Except for programming specifically targeting religious audiences, few mainstream television or film characters explicitly espouse or engender religious beliefs or lifestyles.

As a result, media attention to religion tends to occur during those negative moments when someone or some group abrogates the shared secular sensibility and religion crashes into public view. The attacks of September 11 join such other media spectacles as raids on polygamist Mormon communities, the mass weddings of Reverend Moon's followers, and the suicide of Jim Jones and his Peoples Temple. The price paid by those who challenge the understood place of religion tends to be suspicion regarding their group's legitimacy as a religion. News outlets and their experts often apply labels such as "cult" and "extremists" to differentiate these groups from "normal" religious groups that know to stay within the established lines.

An important distinction usually arises, however, between the depiction of seemingly aberrant forms of Christian traditions and of Muslim ones. At the time when the groups made headlines, the Christian majority of the United States did not consider the Peoples Temple or Branch Davidians as representative of Christian traditions in the same was as many consider al-Qaeda representative of Islamic traditions. When their untimely demise made the followers of Jones and David Koresh the focus of national attention, media spokespeople and the experts upon whom they called unwittingly deflected the possibility of criticism toward Christians in general by describing these groups as "cults" and "pseudo-religions." By challenging the leaders' character with suspicions regarding their political, sexual, and psychological motivations, news outlets provided portrayals of men many in the audience assumed were "not really Christian" or "not really religious." After all, the assumption seemed, real Christians do not act like this. In contrast, much of the public debate among Americans about Islamic traditions in the past decade has centered on whether or not "Islam" is implicitly a religion of violence. Hence, non-Muslim Americans have been far less likely to pose the question of whether or not the 9/11 hijackers were "really Muslim" than whether or not they represent a quality inherent to all Islamic traditions. Hence the many calls for "moderate Muslims" to declare their eschewal of these groups, prove their conformity to secular values, or be excluded because their Islamic commitments inherently conflict with American ones.

Overall, therefore, the academic study of religion offers a larger comparative framework in which to understand Muslims and the Islamic traditions they practice. In particular, scholars help elaborate the assumptions made about religion by an overwhelmingly Christian American audience. Despite repeated polls that demonstrate Muslim disapproval for the crimes of September 11 and other acts of terrorism, other polls reflect a deepening suspicion of Islam among non-Muslim Americans. While pollyannish and apologetic reporting on Muslim communities certainly will not assuage hardened Islamophobic and anti-Muslim views, more nuanced approaches that take into account the particular norms of American views on religion in general and Islamic traditions in particular may go a long way to help alleviate the increasing Islamophobia suffered by the nation's Muslim citizens.

Peter Gottschalk is Professor of Religion at Wesleyan University. He is author of *American Heretics: Catholics, Jews, Muslims, and the History of Religious Intolerance* and is coauthor of *Islamophobia: Making Muslims the Enemy.*

FOUR

LIFE AS A MUSLIM IN THE MEDIA

Zarqa Nawaz

MY LIFE AS A WRITER came about in a circuitous route. As a daughter of Pakistani immigrants, the highest career aspiration was to become a medical doctor. It was a stable, well-paying career that had the respect of the wider Muslim community. A career as a writer never entered my mind. Careers that involved film, TV, and newspapers seemed inaccessible to me. For my parents, particularly my father, who had come of age during the partition of India and Pakistan in 1947 and who had lost everything—home, land, money—education was the key for financial security. A future in writing didn't guarantee an income the way a future in medicine did.

It wasn't until I went to Muslim camp as a teenager with my best friend Rahat, who wanted to be a writer, that the idea that Muslims could be something other than doctors entered my mind. I viewed my friend as an exotic creature who was pursuing a career in something akin to the French Foreign Legion. She encouraged me to volunteer for the Muslim camp newsletter and write pieces for it. The editor would insist I change careers from science to media. I'd explain patiently that I wasn't writer material. Writer-type people were cool and sophisticated, and I was a gangly teenager with braces and bad fashion sense. Plus, I was committed to my medical path. But the seed had been planted. Part of the problem was that in the 1980s, very few Muslims went into media while entire hospitals units were staffed with Muslim physicians. You could probably get away with speaking only Urdu in many oncology wards in the country. There simply weren't a lot of role models in the world of journalism to emulate. I decided to stick with the master medical plan while writing for community newsletters and acting badly in plays. And then the year I turned twenty-two, disaster struck. After I finished my four-year bachelor of science degree at the University of Toronto, I was rejected for medical school. It should have been obvious from the start that I was unsuited for a career in the medical world. University had been a difficult time, with classes such as organic chemistry and statistics that remained a total mystery. I would write essays instead of solving physics equations during exams. I had ignored my creative instinct to my own detriment as I found myself floundering, trying to find a career. I felt rudderless. My best friend had always talked about Ryerson Polytechnical Institute's famous school of journalism. My conservative Pakistani mother felt it was time to arrange a marriage to a nice Pakistani boy. It was just the motivation I needed. I phoned Ryerson and found out they were still accepting applications. Given that I had an almost negligible portfolio, I was fortunate that not a lot of students with four-year science degrees were applying to the school. It was a miracle that I was accepted.

FIRSTHAND EXPERIENCE WITH DIVERSITY IN THE MEDIA

When I got in, I was the only Muslim student in my class. But what does it mean to have little representation of a community in news and television? Shouldn't anyone be able to tell another community's stories? There were always rumblings in the community that if we didn't tell our own stories, they would be told for us from another, not always positive perspective. I learned firsthand how vital it was to have a diverse newsroom when I got my first part-time job as a journalism student as a researcher for the *National*, the Canadian Broadcasting Corporation's (CBC's) flagship news show. It was 1990 and the Gulf War had just broken out, and reporters were caught off-guard. I had walked in to do a student interview with David Bazay, the executive producer of the *National*. At that time, there was no one in the newsroom who was Muslim. I was arrogant and full of myself. I told David they were pronouncing Islam and Muslim improperly; my great contribution to journalism was how to sound out a soft "s." But luckily for me, David could see through my pseudo-machismo and decided to hire me to write a research paper about the Muslim community: find out what the breakdown of the Muslim community in Canada was, where were the mosques, what was the Muslim population in each province, who were the imams in the mosques, who were the movers and shakers within each community. I created the document and was told it was a useful tool in the newsroom in the absence of Muslim reporters. Having a diverse newsroom was important, not just so that names could be pronounced correctly, but to understand the different perspectives within the community. The community itself was a diverse group. There was no "Arab Street" or single opinion. It would be like asking an Irish person to speak for all the world's white people.

After working for the CBC news department for a few years, I moved into radio production and worked as a producer for *Morningside*, a morning radio show hosted by the venerable Peter Gzowski. My job was to find people to interview and come up with interview questions for Peter. He would interview the guest using the questions we had come up with and create magic on the air with his deep, melodious voice. It was then that I felt a creative itch that wasn't being fulfilled by journalism anymore. I could feel the world of story calling to me. I was obsessed with Woody Allen movies at the time and how he captured the angst of his Jewish community in these wonderful films. I wanted to do something similar with the Muslim community. But how do you make the jump from journalism to filmmaking? Again, like journalism, filmmaking is one of those careers without a defined path. A teacher at the Ontario College of Art told me to take an introduction to filmmaking course he was teaching in the summer. Each student made a five-minute film about any subject they chose. I signed up right away and found myself thinking about a topic for my first film when the Alfred P. Murrah Federal Building in Oklahoma City was bombed on April 19, 1995, killing 168 people, including 19 children under the age of six. Immediately there were photographs of Muslim suspects in the *Toronto Star*. A few days later, Timothy McVeigh, a Gulf War veteran, was arrested. He had blown up the building in retaliation for the way the US federal government handled the Waco siege. I had been convinced it was a Muslim behind the terrorist bombing by the way the news media was covering the event. I had no idea there were right-wing militia groups in the United States who had been plotting against the government for years. The assumption in the media was that only Muslims could be capable of such violence. I had an epiphany.

SHATTERING STEREOTYPES IN FILM

My first film, *BBQ MUSLIMS*, was born. Two Muslim brothers are sleeping one night and the backyard barbecue blows up. The neighbors turn against them and immediately accuse them of being Middle Eastern terrorists even though they've never left Canada. (Strangely, this turn of events was to happen to our family shortly after 9/11.) The real perpetuators were a group called BARF, the Barbecue Anti-Resistance Front. They were going around blowing up barbecues because of the air pollution they were causing. But they hadn't realized they had blown up a Muslim family's barbecue, and now they couldn't get attention for their cause anymore because the police and the media were obsessing over the innocent brothers. The film was crude and used my family and neighbors who lived nearby. I, of course, was convinced it was Oscar material and sent it to the Toronto International Film Festival for consideration.

A few months later I received a call from one of the organizers. Given the film's grim production values, the organizer admitted that it was a bit of a risk to program the film, but the selection committee couldn't overlook the fact that there weren't a lot of comedic films being made about a difficult topic: Muslims and the stereotypes of terrorism. So instead of becoming the next Woody Allen, making intellectual urban films about neurotic angst, I had found a niche making satirical films about Muslim stereotypes. I decided it was a sign to start my filmmaking career in earnest.

While watching the news, I saw endless stories about Muslims, always angry, always brown, not terribly good-looking and oftentimes bearded, chanting for the death of someone for some egregious violation, firing a gun in the air. (Someone should really do a story about where all those bullets land.) Nuance is always difficult in rapid-fire journalism, but the ubiquitous chanting mullah sound bite reduces the Muslim community to a caricature of the Queen of Hearts in *Alice in Wonderland*, declaring "off with their heads" at every turn. Inspired by these types of stories, I wrote a short comedy titled *Death Threat*, about a young Muslim woman named Yasmeen Siddiqui who is an aspiring writer. She writes a schlocky novel that no publisher is willing to take on. Yasmeen decides that since the media is obsessed with crazy Muslims, she will purposely upset the local Muslim community and coax out a fatwa of death to help promote her book and finally launch her career. Instead of stoning her, though, her community tries to appease her and to figure out how to make her happy. After failing to enrage them, she decides to take a short cut to fame, writes out her own death threat, and tries to get a Muslim leader to sign it. But the only ones who are willing to kill her are two Canadian farmers who feel the government has cut their wheat subsidy and the only way to make up the shortfall is to collect a bounty on a Muslim woman.

Muslim Community's Concerns

It was a pretty crazy film that took quintessential Canadian and Muslim stereotypes and mixed them up. The film itself was a satirical take on the issue of fatwas and Muslims. It was also accepted at the Toronto International Film Festival. Just as I was finishing up my first feature film script, the National Film Board of Canada approached me to submit a proposal for a documentary. At that time, our mosque in Regina, Saskatchewan, had just erected a physical barrier between the men and women in the main prayer hall. There has always been a contentious debate about the role of women in public religious places, and the conservative element of the community felt that women should be behind a wall of some sort. I felt I had the subject for my documentary: the segregation of women in mosques.

There was a great deal of angst from the community about whether I should be "washing our dirty laundry" in public. It was generally felt that the overall impression of our community was so negative in the media that making my documentary would just add fuel to the Islamophobic fire. But to me, the non-Muslim community already had a negative impression of the community, and creating positive propaganda pieces were not going to change attitudes. For me this was an opportunity to deal with a subject that would have been difficult to do in a news segment. There was context, history, religion, culture, and diversity of opinion that had to be dealt with, and an hour-long documentary provided me with enough time to do justice to this subject. I believed that if I exposed the patriarchy behind some of the oppressive practices within the community, it could help create a better understanding of the faith. Since Islam doesn't endorse putting women behind curtains and walls, but some Muslims do, the religion was being tarnished by practice; tradition was being mixed up with theology by Muslims themselves. I wanted to make a documentary that would educate both Muslims and non-Muslims alike. I traveled around North America interviewing various scholars and community members about the issue.

What I found most fascinating about the experience of making this documentary was how willing Muslims were to talk about the issues of patriarchy and misogyny within the mosque structures. It wasn't just the women who were suffering. It was also the husbands, brothers, fathers, and sons who hated the way women were being treated and wanted the community to own up to its shortcomings. And everyone wanted to make it clear that religion was being used to defend unsavory practices. Muslims were tired of having religion being used to prop up essentially misogynistic practices.

The documentary came out and the response was overwhelmingly positive. Many Muslims told me later that they used the documentary as a tool to trigger conversations about how mosques would be structured when they were in the design stage. Non-Muslims told me they appreciated an honest documentary about the issue because they too were experiencing similar attitudes in their own faith communities. Turns out that the controversy of the place of women in faith communities is a universal one. Before I made my documentary, I watched the documentary *Half My Kingdom*, directed by Roushell Goldstein and Francine Zuckerman, about separation and segregation between men and women that occurs in synagogues. Jewish men and women are not stereotyped in the same way that Muslim men and women are and yet there are many parallels in both communities when it comes to patriarchy and how it defines religious practice. In my view, the best way to counter these impressions is to discuss how Islamic feminism is being used to fight oppressive practices that do indeed exist in the community, but to do it from a fair vantage point, which is to put blame on the culture and not the religion.

Little Mosque Is Born

I was asked to participate in the Banff Television Festival in Alberta, Canada, about my experience making the documentary. Up to that point in my career, I was focusing on making independent films and I even had a feature film script to pitch. A young Muslim actor wants to propose to his longtime fiancée. But like a lot of young actors, he's hard up for cash. He accepts a job playing a terrorist about to hijack a plane. His fiancée is hired by the Muslim community to protest against the making of this film because it promotes stereotypes about Muslims. The moment the words "Muslims" and "hijacking a plane" came out of my mouth, producers' faces would go white. It was just five years after 9/11 and sensitivity to the subject was still high. I had one producer tell me I had come up with the worst pitch he had ever heard in his professional career.

Lucky for me, I had come to Banff with another proposal. A good friend of mine had told me that Banff is the place where television series are pitched. With the documentary fresh in my mind, I felt that mosques had the potential to be different places if the imam came from a culture where gender equity was a priority and that a proper understanding of faith would result in a mosque with proper access for women to the prayer hall as well as the power structure. I came up with a pitch where a young Toronto lawyer named Amaar Rashid decides to give up his law degree and become an imam of a small, broken-down mosque in Mercy, Saskatchewan. He gets embroiled in the usual gender issues of the community, and he finds it challenging taking sides since he has to represent his entire congregation. To my surprise, this pitch was instantly popular and people paid attention. Of course, I was heartbroken that no one wanted my "Muslim hijacks a plane" pitch, but an imam dealing with contemporary issues in a Canadian mosque was what everyone preferred.

What was important to me was not to create a show that showed Muslims as horrible misogynist monsters or Muslims as totally misunderstood crusaders of gender equity. The truth lies somewhere in between. Sexism, racism, and extremism are part of the Muslim community as much as they are part of other faith communities, and I didn't want to shy away from dealing with these subjects. But they also didn't define us. We are husbands and wives and children. We are ordinary people, with jobs and mortgages and concerns about where are kids are going to school, who is going to unplug the toilet and unload the dishwasher. But the Muslim community has morphed into the "other," and our humanness has disappeared. I wanted a show to give us back our humanity, warts and all.

The show aired to spectacular ratings. The media attention around the world was overwhelming. More than one reporter told me this was the first time a Muslim had been depicted in a bland way, which was the biggest compliment for me. "Muslims can be boring too" should have been my slogan.

There were seven main Muslim characters in *Little Mosque on the Prairie*, some practicing, some not. The idea was to reflect the diversity of the Muslim community. I had underestimated the media attention that a series like this would generate. In retrospect, it made sense because there had never been a mainstream comedy about a Muslim family like there had been with other minority groups, such as African Americans on *The Cosby Show*. If the first North American Muslim sitcom had been about a Muslim family, I think there would have been less publicity, but the first Muslim sitcom was set in a mosque, not a living room.

There were no baby steps to prepare the non-Muslim and Muslim communities for this new show. Non-Muslims probably expected the same violence that came when the Danish cartoon controversy broke out in 2005, where Muslims became violent because they were upset about the perceived blasphemous cartoons of the prophet. I remember the endless stream of interviews from the *New York Times* to *Al-Jazeera* to the BBC. As a result of this speculation of "What Were The Muslims Going to Do?" the CBC got unprecedented media coverage that the publicity budget would never have been able to buy. Historically it's been difficult for Canadian television shows to compete with American shows because the Americans have vastly more advertising dollars. As a result of the substantial media publicity, *Little Mosque on the Prairie* debuted to record-breaking ratings. Ironically this success would not have been possible without the level of scrutiny the community was under after 9/11. I did an interview with Glenn Beck, then working for CNN, about *Little Mosque on the Prairie*. He was concerned about the Muslim community not having a sense of humor about Islam and becoming potentially violent. To be fair, there were some Muslims who made me wonder if they did have a sense of humor and were unhappy with the show. But they either wrote to the CBC or to me, or they signed a petition with other signatories to express their dislike of the show rather than throw a Molotov cocktail at my house, which was a relief.

A Personal Reflection of Culture and Beliefs

I am a Canadian of Muslim faith, so *Little Mosque on the Prairie* reflected both my Canadian culture and my Islamic beliefs, which meant that people who didn't share my cultural upbringing but shared my religious upbringing found certain aspects of the show unsettling. For example, the episode that had Muslims participating in Halloween was controversial in that some Muslims felt that Halloween wasn't a common holiday in their home country and had aspects of pagan rituals associated with its origins, which made it Islamically questionable. I was familiar with the controversy so I dealt with the subject by making Halloween about the candy and community camaraderie. For me, the show was an interesting way to create dialogue between the first and second generation of Muslims while helping non-Muslims understand some of the cultural nuances of the community. The second generation of Muslims, who grew up in North America, understood and reacted positively to *Little Mosque on the Prairie*, while their parents had a much more difficult time with it. I remember the president of the Islamic Association of Saskatchewan, who was from Indonesia, telling me his son laughed while watching the show. He was worried that the show was mocking Islam, but he couldn't be sure since he didn't really understand what the characters were saying.

The criticism I heard constantly over the years from the first-generation Muslim community, particularly from the conservative element, was that I should make each and every Muslim on *Little Mosque on the Prairie* perfect in every way in order to give a better impression of Islam. As if non-Muslim opinion about Muslims would miraculously change if there was a sitcom in which Muslims appeared in a perfect, unblemished light. The irony is that people respect us more when we are honest about our shortcomings instead of pretending they don't exist. I heard interesting comments from religious people from other faith communities who told me that their places of worship had the same mix of congregants—the hypocritical elder, the rebellious teenager, the fence sitter, the matriarch, etc. The characters on *Little Mosque on the Prairie* were universal and relatable, which is what I believe made it successful for a diverse international audience. The only new thing about it was that it was set in a mosque with Muslim characters.

For sure, there is a skewed perception of Muslims in the news, especially networks such as Fox News, which tend to portray Islam in a negative light. Ironically, the character of Baber, the conservative, rigid Muslim, was the most beloved character in the show. He was always trying to prove he was the best Muslim, and his schemes often misfired. I was often asked to make him less stupid, more serious-minded, and less fun by the very Muslims who inspired him in the first place. This would have resulted only in the show getting canceled, but conservative Muslims honestly felt I was ruining the image of a good Muslim man. Amaar, the imam, wasn't considered an appropriate imam by conservative Muslims because he didn't have a beard. Ironically, non-Muslims loved Baber and he was probably their favorite Muslim character.

It was confusing to me at first but I realized that Baber helped humanize the stereotype of a severe, fundamentalist Muslim man. He gave that stereotype more nuance by being a single father raising a daughter by himself. Especially since that daughter didn't practice Islam the way he wanted it practiced. Instead of demanding she wear hijab, he was gentle and kind toward her, saw things from his daughter's perspective, and never forced her to do things she didn't want to do. I recall a radio interview I did in the United States when an American caller phoned in. He told me he could never look at a bearded Muslim man in the same way again. I found this comment interesting. I had never intended for *Little Mosque on the Prairie* to be a propaganda piece for the local Muslim community. I fully intended to show Muslims with all their numerous flaws, which some Muslims took umbrage to, but as a result of this depiction, non-Muslims seemed to have a better opinion of Islam despite the constant refrain from conservative Muslims that I was giving the wrong image of Islam. There were two nonhijabis (Sarah and Layla) and two hijabis (Rayann and Fatima) to reflect the realities of Muslim women today.

For some non-Muslims, the only exposure they had to Muslims was watching *Little Mosque on the Prairie*, and everything they learned about Islam came through the show. On the surface, that's a disturbing sentiment since the show was never supposed to be an Islam 101 course, but the fact that it became a source of this knowledge meant it also had a chance to provide an alternative to the current media image of Islam, which depicts Muslims behaving unjustly, particularly when it comes to women. In fact, it seemed that it had won over a sizeable audience among Muslims, who could now take the occasional criticisms of the community in stride.

It's interesting also to note the differences between the Canadian response to *Little Mosque on the Prairie* and the American response. I have been almost exclusively invited to speak at American Muslim Student Association conferences, universities, and Muslim and non-Muslim events. I believe this has to do with the attacks on US citizens on 9/11. The American Muslim community has suffered a great deal of discrimination after the attacks, and as a result the American Muslim community has become much more civic-minded and engaged in community altruism than before the attacks. They want to present themselves as a force of good in society and counter the negative publicity the attacks brought to Islam and Muslims. They view *Little Mosque on the Prairie* as an alternative view of the Muslim community from the one shown on American television, such as *24*, *Homeland*, and Fox News.

When the *Little Mosque on the Prairie* first aired, I was accused by both right-wing Muslims and non-Muslims of wanting to change the image of Islam to my version. Right-wing non-Muslim commentators have suggested that I created *Little Mosque on the Prairie* as propaganda to whitewash the image of Islam so that the Muslim community could be trusted again, thus making it easier for Muslims to plan another attack on North America. I was showing a version of Islam that wasn't angry and hateful and violent and therefore did not represent real Islam. To right-wing Muslims, I was showing a version of Islam that they claimed included feminism, participation in Western practices such as Halloween, allowing a beardless imam, allowing women a greater voice and presence in the mosque and community, etc. Thus I was showing a version of Islam that wasn't strict, did not respect their authority, and did not condemn everything they condemned and therefore wasn't the real Islam. It's interesting to note that both Muslim and non-Muslim right-wing groups were united in their hatred in the show for basically the same reason: it wasn't their version of Islam. In the end, the show was my version of Islam and how I perceived the community.

It shouldn't come as a surprise that the American Muslim community is still perceived in a negative light. The result of the endless cycle of negative new stories is very real Islamophobia. In 2014, the Pew Research and Public Life Center did a survey of Americans' feelings about different religious groups. They found that Muslims were at the bottom of all religious categories. These negative feelings can affect a community as it attempts to assimilate into the wider community. Activities such as building new mosques to running for political office can become mired in suspicion and negativity.

Making assumptions about Muslims can be damaging, such as the belief that hijab is an oppressive piece of clothing. Some Muslim women wear the hijab, some wear the niqab, some don't wear any of the identifying features. Why are these garments worn? What do they mean to individual women? And for some women, wearing different types of religious dress are expressions on faith, and they go through their own journeys of self-discovery. It would be like saying that wearing high heels and miniskirts objectifies white women and therefore they should be banned from wearing them. Every woman has the right to choose what she wears regardless of her faith because she has agency, but in the case of Muslim women it is sometimes assumed that she cannot make a choice that's best for her.

Attitudes of intolerance can culminate in discriminatory laws such as the antihijab legislation passed in many countries in Europe, such as France, which banned the wearing of hijab for girls who want to attend high school. These laws cause communities to feel alienated and are hurtful to the very girls the laws are trying to protect. Some of the girls leave the education system for private Islamic schools that may have substandard education, which results in fewer opportunities for the future.

Ultimately, the antidote to the problem of Islamophobia lies within all of us.

Stories about the Muslim community should be fair and accurate without demonizing an entire people. My advice to anyone writing a story about the community is to reach out to a diverse group of Muslims and get a wider perspective on an issue. Stereotypes about the community should be challenged with informed reporting. The Muslim diaspora is a vital part of the American landscape, and stories that showcase the full experience of the community can only benefit all of us.

> Zarqa Nawaz created *Little Mosque on the Prairie*, the world's first sitcom about a Muslim community living in the West. She is author of *Laughing All the Way to the Mosque* and is a frequent public speaker on Islam and comedy, gender and faith, and diversity in the media.

FIVE

THE PRISONS OF PARADIGM

Rafia Zakaria

IF THE GLOBAL PUBLIC SPHERE were a giant stage and writing about Muslim women a global morality play with its principal characters allotted roles of the most good and the most evil, the Muslim woman, as it were, would be given the part of the silent, suffering victim, that hapless soul for whose rescue or subjugation the good and the bad contend and in the contrast of whose depravity and nobility the cathartic value of the exchange depends. In contemporary castings, parts of the noble avenger may be allotted variously to the white, already-liberated feminists and even NATO soldiers; the part of the evil villain would be generally played by Muslim men. The subject of rescue, for the sake of visual familiarity, may be clad in a black abaya or a blue burka, variously subjugated by tribal rite or religious custom; she is often nameless and featureless (or with appendages variously hacked) and almost never delivers any dialogue.

The value of imagining the global public sphere in this dimension is that it reveals a paradigm variously contributed to by history and politics, orientalism and colonialism, to produce the frame through which Muslim women are viewed in the hundreds of thousands of articles and essays and news clips and tweets produced in a real-time world. The producers of the play, the selectors of the cast, in charge of dramatizing the parts and conjuring the costumes, are in general Westerners, whose media and frames dominate the discourse of the global public sphere. The play is performed in numerous contexts and for varied audiences. In the context of recent wars, the invasions of Afghanistan and Iraq both utilized the familiar dimensions of its moral oppositions to cast US soldiers as the avengers of Muslim women, the harbingers of liberty, and providers of equality. The denouement of the play could be simple or complicated. It could be a platoon of soldiers bringing boxes of books to a desolate dusty village in the gray crags of Afghanistan, or soldiers can fight off or cajole disapproving elders or marauding bands of Taliban for a school for wordless women who appear in final shots, delivering silent, smiling gratitude.

Muslim Women and Western Feminism

In the context of Western feminism, the plot is only slightly altered. A white woman, an aid worker, a cosmetologist, or a nurse penetrates the secret worlds of Muslim women—a village or a beauty shop[1] or the female quarters of a warlord—and then teaches and inspires them to throw off the shackles of their segregated, subjugated existence by taking on the brutes that force them to be kept apart. The hero in the story is now female, but still Western, sympathetic, and stalwart, taking on the starring role, keeping the loudest and noblest voice for herself. She takes down the system, challenges the order, and makes the suffering of the women legible to her aghast but admiring audience. If the theme of school-building soldiers was war, the theme in this feature is compassionate, benevolent assistance that glibly, smugly keeps quiet about the denominators of power and the necessity of the subjugated in emphasizing the heroism of the Western avenger.

There is much laid bare here. The delicate differences in the casting of the good soldier and the well-meaning white feminist, as radically different as the two characters may be, indicates how the differences in their politics,[2] their positions of war, and their prioritization of the welfare of women are dulled in their juxtaposition against Muslim women as the ultimate other, on whose saving their own moral goodness axiomatically and paradigmatically depends. In the particularities of Western politics, in fact, they may lie on divergent ends of the political spectrum, the first most emblematically represented by the Bush administration's avowals at the onset of the wars in Iraq and Afghanistan that pivoted war efforts on the backs of spreading gender equality.[3] The second may come from liberal feminists, a constituency most opposed to the first, opposed to war but yet utilizing the same paradigm to celebrate their own gains.

FRAMING GOOD AND EVIL MUSLIMS

The other dimension to the morality play paradigm is its own inherent and structural reliance on emphasizing the difference between the good and the evil. In the context of Muslim women—whether the topic may be an honor killing in Canada[4] where an irate Muslim father, angry at his daughter's interest in the opposite sex, tries to kill her for dishonoring him, or a case of spousal abuse in Jordan where a woman's husband disfigured her permanently when she asked for a divorce—the helplessness of the victim underscores both the evil of the perpetrator and the goodness of those who speak out against him. For the journalist reporting on either story, the challenges are twofold; first are the prerogatives of a good story, where the moral elements of good and bad, which give interest and impetus to the tale, are dulled by the complexities of context. Context added here runs up against the crush of both the word limit and the structural demands of a good story.

In simple terms, how much of an overarching explanation of the immigrant culture of Muslims in Canada, the discrimination faced by Muslim men regularly profiled as terrorists, must a journalist reporting on a story add to his or her piece? And how indeed must the attractions of adding sensation by fitting into existing paradigms, those magical themes that attract the reader, be sacrificed? Viewed in these terms, the challenges for balanced reporting on Muslim women, which refuses to cast her in the role of silent sufferer, is that the addition of context often seems like justification, the blurring of moral lines that sneaks too close to relativism, producing an uncomfortable or ambiguous account, unpleasing to editors and unattractive to readers.

The second challenge is simply one of reporting the truth. Take for instance a story run by *TIME* magazine on its cover on August 4, 2010.[5] The story featured a young eighteen-year-old Afghan girl by the name of Bibi Aisha who had her nose cut off and had taken refuge in an Afghan shelter for ten months before being sent (courtesy of the reporter who found her) to a hospital in the West for reconstructive surgery. The girl herself could not read or write, did not speak English, and had never heard of *TIME* magazine prior to having her picture taken for the cover. The caption next to her face read "What happens when we leave Afghanistan." In relation to our discussion here, the question posed from the perspective of truth would insist that there was absolutely nothing wrong with putting Bibi Aisha's face on the cover of the magazine. It was indeed true that she lost her nose in a horrendous act of misogyny, that she took refuge in a shelter, and that she consented to have her disfigured face presented to the world. Each one of these facts is true, and if the duty of the journalist is defined solely as reporting the truth, then indeed the cast and character of the *TIME* story accomplished the purpose.

In sum, then, the prerogatives of a good story, of an aversion to moral relativism and a commitment to truth, all seem to point to presenting the Muslim woman as Bibi Aisha was on the *TIME* cover or as the silent victim of honor killings in Canada or the secretly happy student of an Afghan village school built by American soldiers. The challenge and entrenchment of the paradigm, its persistence, is that for Westerners and Western journalists alike it is difficult to retell the story without relying on the morality play as the model. A departure from it represents the absence of a marked plot, the uncertain dimensions of unearthing a new one, the ambiguity of a cast where none of the characters are familiar, where the dimensions of what must be thought—and even further of what must be done—are consequently murky and unclear.

Framing Muslim Women: A Moral Challenge

The prison of paradigm, with respect to the Muslim woman as she emerges in Western media, is thus revealed as a moral challenge, where definitions of empirical fact and moral truth are all put to issue when the task of changing the paradigm is confronted. The "real" stories of Muslim women, the everyday stories of women who go to work even if they are forced to wear burkas or who compete at sports events with their heads covered in hijab, are rarely reported, not simply because of a lack of interest, but because the moral constructs of the Western world rely on the silence or submission of those variously referred Eastern/Muslim/Arab women to highlight the liberation and freedom of Western women. In male equations, the civilized goodness of the American soldier relies on the barbarism of the Afghan father or brother or husband who would hack off a nose or sell off a sister for a plot of land or a bunch of goats. To ask for a different kind of reporting is to ask journalists to abandon what sells, what feels right, and ultimately what provides the reader a clear and accessible point of moral identification, sympathy for a victim, veneration for the soldier/liberator, and anger at the barbaric and evil perpetrator.

I began this essay using the analogy of a morality play to describe the roles and paradigms constricting the portrayal of Muslim women in news reporting and the wider media. My intent in doing this was simple: many essays can point out with a plethora of examples—from popular culture, television, web-based media, and others—the typecasting of Muslim women into the roles of the silent, subjugated subject. I could also have used the work of notable Muslim feminist scholars such as Fatima Mernissi, Leila Ahmed, Laleh Bakhtiar, and a host of others to emphasize how the constructs of Orientalist framing, from the harem to the burka, have for centuries governed the dynamics of this presentation. I could, as many of these scholars have done, and as is the case, highlighted the work and stories of brave Muslim women throughout history who have challenged tradition and assumed positions of leadership. All those approaches are valid substantive approaches to the issue, but enumerating these successes, while both crucial and valuable, does not address the purported ethical and moral obstacles that cause these paradigms to persist within the Western imagination and hence in journalistic accounts about Muslim women.

To enunciate a paradigm is ultimately to begin to forge a path to defeat it. In presenting the reasons why the construct of the subjugated Muslim woman persists, I have attempted to present an agenda for the basis of understanding what needs to be changed in order for a more prescient and multidimensional picture of the Muslim woman to emerge in journalistic writing. First among these would be a reprioritization of journalistic values such as the dislocation of an existing paradigm, one that limits perception of the Western journalist and the Western reader so that they see only stories with familiar characters or are redolent with comfortable angles. In this sense, the rejection of the paradigm must be seen as a value that would enable more truthful reporting, a more varied and richer picture, than the tropes of old. In the case of Bibi Aisha, the girl on the cover of *TIME*, the caption to the photo would, with the use of these new standards, have read not "What happens if we leave" but rather "What has happened while we were there."

Rafia Zakaria is an attorney, human rights activist, and writer. She is author of *The Upstairs Wife: An Intimate History of Pakistan*. Her columns have appeared in the *Guardian*, on Dawn.com, and in the *Baffler*.

SIX

UNVEILING OBSESSIONS: MUSLIMS AND THE TRAP OF REPRESENTATION

Nabil Echchaibi

IN MAY 2012, THE *NEW YORK TIMES* published yet again another feature article about veiling in Iran. "Your Veil Is a Battleground" showcases the work of Iranian-born photographer Kiana Hayeri as she reflects on dress and public life among young women in Iran. Through a captivating photographic slideshow that reveals the hidden life of Iranian women veiled and without clothing, the article makes the now trite but romantic argument that behind the veil lies a secret world of social transgressions and a yearning for individual freedom. "Ms. Hayeri," the article reads, "returned to Iran in 2010 to explore the dual lives of many young women who are expected to behave and dress modestly in public by covering their hair, arms and legs. But behind closed doors, these women act very much like Ms. Hayeri's Canadian friends—dating, singing, studying ballet and even swimming."[1] It is obvious that the motive behind Hayeri's excellent photography is to capture a rarely seen facet of Iranian private life, but its import bears a somber resemblance to the unveiling obsession that has plagued popular representations of Islam and Muslims since the romantic orientalism of Delacroix's harem paintings in North Africa. The penetrating secrecy of Hayeri's pictures evokes multiple scenes and narratives—at times easily discernible—of uncloaking the mystery of Islam and the intimacy of Muslim life: the dramatic televised unveiling act of 2001 when Oprah lifted the burka off an Afghani woman on stage amid the roaring chants of an all-female audience;

that trifling scene from the 2010 blockbuster *Sex and the City 2* when a group of niqabi women speak for the first time when they take off their veils and reveal stylish Western clothing and shoes just like models fantasizing about parading in a New York City fashion show; the highly publicized controversy over the building of an Islamic cultural center near Ground Zero in New York City, which quickly morphed into a discussion about the suspicious and secretive world of Muslims inside their mosques; or the cancelled reality television show *All-American Muslim*, which supposedly took American audiences "inside the rarely seen world of American Muslims to uncover a unique community struggling to balance faith and nationality in a post 9/11 world."

Surely lumping these examples together risks trivializing important differences in their motives and the subjective position of their authors, but they are indicative of an enduring representational trope or trap that forces Islam and Muslims to be perpetual objects of scrutiny who need to prove their normalcy and unveil their hidden lives. This chapter offers some reflections on what I call the "double burden of Muslim representation" and what it means for the possibility of shifting the discourse away from narratives of salvation and unveiling. I argue that a necessary politics of compensation by Muslims and non-Muslims alike is contributing to a culture that constantly tries to recuperate a Muslim worldview. Through observations from the author's work directing a research project on Muslims in the Mountain West, this chapter will also reflect on whether Muslims can absolve themselves of this burden by making their marginality a productive space of articulating their American difference.

BITTER, DEFENSIVE MUSLIMS AND THE BURDEN OF REPRESENTATION

In 2010, a *Newsweek* cover showing a hazy and harrowing picture of the ruins of the World Trade Center asks whether a Muslim imam and his organization's plan to build an Islamic cultural center near the hallowed space of Ground Zero was an insensitive provocation. The cover story chronicled the remarkably churlish response that the idea of an Islamic building, largely perceived only as a mosque, had generated among politicians, intellectuals, and ordinary Americans. Republican Newt Gingrich, a candidate in the

2012 Republican primaries, led the charge against the building proposal, equating it with a creeping furtive plan whose sole purpose was Islamic triumphalism on American soil: "They say they're interfaith, but they didn't propose the building of a mosque, church and synagogue. Instead they proposed a 13-story mosque and community center that will extol the glories of Islamic tolerance for people of other faiths, all while overlooking the site where radical Islamists killed almost 3,000 people in a shocking act of hatred. Building this structure on the edge of the battlefield created by radical Islamists is not a celebration of religious pluralism and mutual tolerance; it is a political statement of shocking arrogance and hypocrisy."[2]

Implicit in Gingrich's warning, which prompted slogans such as "Islam builds mosques on the sites of their conquests" and "All I need to know about Islam I learned on 9/11," is the imminence of the Islamic peril and the steadfastness of Muslims, including Muslim Americans, in their quest to recreate an Islamic state in the United States. Gingrich did not have to invent this narrative of fear and suspicion. That script had been carefully prepared by a coterie of anti-Islam activists who wrote books and kept prolific blogs cautioning Americans against the dangerous maneuvers of deceptively peaceful Muslims. Overnight, the authors of heretofore marginal anti-Islam rhetoric became favorite guests on television programs and frequent sources in newspaper and magazine articles, lending undue visibility in mainstream discourse to a long-standing narrative of Islam bashing.[3]

The sensational reaction to the "Ground Zero mosque" controversy, as it was dubbed by its opponents—which included a Florida pastor who called for the public burning of the Qur'an, a campaign against the application of sharia law in US courts, and calls against minimizing the threat of Islam in US public school textbooks—further evoked the lack of transparency about Islam and the suspicious motives of its pious adherents. As became common practice in the post-9/11 coverage of Islam in American mainstream media, reporters eagerly turned to either pious Muslims to defend themselves against accusations of an Islamic takeover or to Muslim renegades to provide an insider's perspective as to the real motive behind the construction of a cultural center near Ground Zero. An articulate Muslim apostate such as Ayaan Hirsi Ali, a Somali-born critic of Islam and a frequent and authoritative source in American news media, carries with her, beyond the right of criticism, the verification of suspicion and the critical testimony of the ex-Muslim or the insider against the concealed danger behind "modern well-meaning" Muslims.

The imam at the heart of the controversy suddenly became the object of fierce scrutiny, and accordingly all his media appearances were defensive and uptight. Even his liberal supporters had to distance him from the rest of Muslims by highlighting his Sufi beliefs as different and more peaceful than the radical ideologies of Sunni Islam. Catchy headlines at the height of the controversy did little to help allay public fear of what goes on inside the world of Muslims: "What Goes On Inside Your Neighborhood Mosque" (NPR); "War Over Ground Zero" (*Newsweek*); "Ground Zero Muslim Center May Get Public Financing" (Reuters); "Obama Supports 'the Right' for Ground Zero Mosque" (AP). Not all news organizations used the Ground Zero mosque shorthand uncritically, but the fact that many headlines did only reinforced the narrative of suspicion that Muslims are often asked to defend themselves against.

It is one thing when this kind of obsessive concern about the secrecy of Islam is contained within a fringe culture and quite another when it freely pervades media discourse and policy circles. One prime example of the prominence of this narrative of distrust came from Samuel Huntington, the author of the well-cited thesis of the "clash of civilizations" and a major influence on foreign policy during the Bush administration. Huntington's Hobbesian classification of the post–Cold War world into cultural blocks defined by irredeemable civilizational divisions singled out Islam or the "Muslim world" as posing a particularly grave threat to Western culture no matter how its faithful appear to be invested in Western consumption patterns and popular culture. He writes: "The essence of Western civilization is the Magna Carta, not the Magna Mac. The fact that non-Westerners may bite into the latter has no implications for their accepting the former. . . . It also has no implications for their attitudes toward the West. Somewhere in the Middle East a half-dozen young men could well be dressed in jeans, drinking Coke, listening to rap, and, between their bows to Mecca, putting together a bomb to blow up an American airliner."[4]

It has become formulaic and predictable to mention Huntington in any writing on foreign policy and Islam, but I insist on using his thesis here to underline the insurmountable pressure placed on American Muslims whenever they get a chance to speak on behalf of their faith. The first order of business, even when reporters don't specifically ask for it, is to distance oneself from public accusations of violence and secrecy and painstakingly attempt to restore some form of peaceful normalcy to the Islamic community. Obviously, the upshot of this checkered mediated presence readily confers on Muslims a perennial image of Islam as a particularly intractable problem despite strong evidence that supports a remarkable sociocultural and economic integration of American Muslims.[5]

This constant scrutinizing spotlight on Islam has also turned some Muslims into at times angry, defensive spokespeople whose appearance in the media often seems like defense testimony on the witness stand. It does not matter what event Muslims are invited to weigh in on, the essence of their contribution is often reduced to a platitude that Islam is a religion of peace that has been hijacked by a tiny faction of extremists. Muslim individuals and advocacy organizations populate television sets and newspaper columns mostly around controversial issues such as the Dubai US ports management controversy in 2006, the Danish cartoons story in 2006, the runaway Muslim convert to Christianity in Florida in 2009, the Fort Hood shooting in 2009, the arrest of a few Muslim Americans on charges of domestic terrorism in 2009, the "Ground Zero mosque" controversy in 2010, the congressional hearings on radical Islam in 2011, the move to ban sharia law by a dozen American states in 2011, and even more so around the rise of the so-called Islamic State or Daesh.

The concentration of Muslim voices around the coverage of these high-profile and incendiary issues has not only made the visibility of Islam contingent on problematic events but has also compelled Muslims to accept the role of the apologetic and bitter faithful who constantly complain about the simplistic and reductionist portrayal of their religion in public discourse. And American Muslim organizations such as the Council of American Islamic Relations (CAIR) and Muslim Public Affairs Council (MPAC), among many others, have become quite adept at dispatching their advocates for this very purpose. CAIR, a grassroots civil rights and advocacy group, has won a series of legal battles since its inception in 1994, mostly on issues of unfair media representation and defending the constitutional rights of American Muslims. MPAC, a public policy and advocacy organization based in Los Angeles, set up a Hollywood bureau in 2007 to "serve as resource in developing multi-dimensional portrayals of Islam and Muslims, and create inroads for aspiring Muslim artists." A number of American Muslims have also created blogs and websites to counter what they perceive as a rampant vilification of their faith and their fellow Muslims in public discourse.[6]

The point here is not to discredit the important work these organizations and Muslim individuals have been doing to ensure more equitable coverage of Islam, but to note that their visibility is largely embedded in a vapid discourse that keeps their work a captive of rigid associations of Muslim men and violence, veiling and women's submission, Islamic law and a Muslim takeover, and Islamic tradition as a reaction to modernity, even when their primary mission is to fight these media caricatures. But the marginality of Muslims in shaping public discourse makes this configuration of a conditional media presence inevitable. This is what I call a "double burden of representation," which sees Muslims compelled to defend their faith and their fellow believers but only from a narrow media agenda that leaves little room for any discursive flexibility. The equation of Islam and violence/extremism is inescapable, and Muslim intervention is made possible mostly from within the confines of this equation, to guard against sweeping generalizations and still prove their loyalty to the United States, as is evident in the recent Muslim American Declaration, a pledge signed by a number of Muslim artists, activists, and intellectuals to commemorate the tenth anniversary of 9/11:

> We are Muslim Americans. We are American Muslims. We live as your neighbors, friends, doctors, lawyers, police officers, soldiers, cab drivers, newspaper vendors, teammates, co-workers, and family—seamlessly and without conflict. We are fully immersed in the American mosaic, and we are proud. . . . Our faith teaches us to be honest, hard-working, productive members of society. Compassion and ethical living are core foundations of our beliefs and an integral part of American character. We ask of ourselves what we ask of others, we seek the good in and for everyone and strive to be well intentioned in our endeavors.[7]

Similarly, and on the same occasion, MPAC presented the White House with "Our Narrative, Our Civic Responsibilities," a declaration by young Muslim American leaders: "Here, we wish to declare our shared commitment to civic engagement in our communities and throughout our nation as a whole. In order to advance a more perfect union, we reaffirm our pledge to uphold the Constitution. This reaffirmation is the underpinning of our declaration to build bridges of understanding, develop a common vision of compassion, and partner with other civic groups to promote America's prosperity. This ensures that we are part of the solution so that America remains a vibrant, pluralistic democracy."[8]

The fact that some of the most prominent Muslim Americans deemed it necessary to still draft and sign these declarations of "proof of American-ness" ten years after the events of 9/11 is evidence that any changes in public perceptions of Islam and Muslims still require laborious struggles. Muslim Americans speak—or are given the right to speak—around the same issues that heighten their religious and cultural difference in a society still struggling to accept Islam as an integral part of its religious landscape. This inevitable insistence on proving loyalty also feeds the secrecy narrative described above in this chapter, as Muslims feel the obligation, and understandably so, to reveal and publicize their real intentions and motives as good, civically committed Americans.

But this burden of proof comes with a high price because both Muslims and journalists seeking their input reify a rigid mark of difference that allows Muslims to speak only from a religious vantage point, even when their work does not necessarily articulate a religious perspective. Of course, Muslims do not intend their differences to be divisive and mutually exclusive, as is clear in the text of the two declarations above, but the restricting ways in which the label "Muslim" is deployed makes them vulnerable to this kind of visible essentialism. Through the work of multiple organizations and media-savvy individuals, American Muslims have developed a creative public presence, but as I will argue in the next section, their identity is addressed only through the religious, turning them into perpetual religious subjects.

MUSLIMS, SELF-ESSENTIALISM, AND THE RELIGIOUS LABEL

In the past few years, American Muslims have identified the media as an important cultural and ideological space of intervention because that is where public perceptions about Islam and Muslims are made and reproduced. Mainstream media are also slowly seeking diverse Muslim voices to counterbalance the lingering narrative of violence and extremism they themselves have helped establish. But in the process, both interventions have produced essentialized archetypes of good versus bad Muslims who both speak only from a vantage point of piety. Accounts of the Muslim stand-up comic, the Muslim rock star, the Muslim sitcom, the Muslim athlete, the Muslim scientist, the Muslim country singer, the Muslim playwright, dominate this shifting discourse and effectively present a more complex view of Muslim identities and realities. The perception the framing label "Muslim" creates, however, becomes a stubborn marker of difference that exclusively defines the cultural production of individuals who also happen to be Muslim. Just like alternative "good" American Muslim voices are made visible only to interrupt a hegemonic narrative of Islamic terrorism, veiling and women's rights, and sharia law versus democracy, this politics of assertive religious identification has become an important and only window of expression for some. And for those who see their religious identity only in relational terms, this normative frame becomes harder to avoid in a post-9/11 discourse, where the religious pervades our thinking around identity politics.

Obviously, identities are not made in a social vacuum, and American Muslims live out their identities in a politically charged context where their faith is a totalizing trope against which all is measured. In their attempt to create meaningful spaces of intervention, American Muslims slowly penetrate public culture to challenge dominant cultural politics. Though still largely peripheral compared to the broader mainstream, a new generation of artists, journalists, politicians, and theologians are adopting a media-savvy strategy that identifies the cultural and political stage as a critical site of contestation. The dramatic testimony of Keith Ellison, the first Muslim US congressman from Minnesota, during the public congressional hearings on Islamic radicalism in 2011 is a good case in point. So is the work of initiatives like MOST (Muslims on Screen and Television), which provides in-depth Muslim roles and story lines to mainstream producers and writers in Hollywood and the television and video game industries, or the media expertise provided by BoomGen Studios, a production company based in New York and Los Angeles, which recently produced the much-hyped reality television program *All-American Muslim* on the TLC network.[9]

Despite the important legwork achieved by such initiatives, the way they appear in the cultural imaginary of American society is primarily as an effort by a religious minority to explain itself and align the tenets of its faith with a modern society. This in itself is an important political project, but it is increasingly inscribed in a normative frame of what is allowable as "Muslim." One of the strongest and well-publicized criticisms of the *All-American Muslim* television program has been its focus on "moderate" Muslims and its failure to draw a "real" portrait of Islam as a religion of fanatical extremism. By veering slightly from the archetypal Muslim stereotype, although the show still had to deal with the classical issues of veiling and unrelenting religious traditions, the program offered audiences a complex range of different Muslim subjectivities, some not religious at all, but the problem was that the heavily politicized label "Muslim" in mainstream discourse ultimately denied these Muslims the ability to articulate the full spectrum of their Americanness away from the exclusive frame of the religious. Even when Shadia, one of the female cast members, insists she doesn't "look Muslim"— she doesn't wear the veil, has a tattoo, and dates outside of her religion—the show still fixates on veiling as a prerequisite for a woman's piety and presents her "rebellion" as an anomaly in the Muslim community. This reaction to the show was also underpinned by a marketing strategy from both the producers and the television network that deliberately exploited the Muslim label and heightened the religious dimension of the show to maximize its ratings and justify its popularity to an advertising base.

Consider also the work of stand-up comedian Maz Jobrani, an Iranian-born actor who grew up in Los Angeles and was cast for years in the role of a Muslim terrorist in Hollywood blockbusters. His comedy routines are both tragic and funny because they engage in a creative interplay between the negative social baggage of Islam and the reality of living as a Muslim in America. Stand-up comedy has become indeed a distinct Muslim cultural expression that introduces Muslim marginal voices to mainstream America. Comedians draw on their personal experience to comment on the terms of their marginality in contemporary American culture. Yet their work is often tagged "Muslim" comedy, underscoring its cultural distinctiveness as a new marketable genre. Jobrani and other comedians have themselves benefited from this labeling because it has allowed them to create a successful niche market for their work even if the terms of their usage of the label "Muslim" is more expansive than its clichéd meaning. But the religious identification, as strategic as it can be, also prevents Muslim subjects from portraying themselves outside of this dominant frame. Some comedians try to resist this classification but find it harder to find venues without it, as British comedian Shazia Mirza commented on being introduced to her audience in the United States as the first ever Muslim female stand-up comedian from Britain. "I just want to be a comedian. I don't want to be a brown comedian, an Asian comedian, a Muslim comedian, I want to just be a comedian who makes people laugh."[10]

In fact, the irony of highlighting the cultural production of American Muslims is that it cannot be done without referring to it as Muslim or without Muslims engaging themselves in some degree of strategic essentialism. One could also argue that when these Muslim narratives enter the marketplace, it is generally a productive way of engaging rather than neutralizing difference. But as Stuart Hall cautions, "Difference, like representation, is also a slippery, and therefore, contested concept. There is the 'difference' which makes a radical and unbridgeable separation: and there is a 'difference' which is positional, conditional and conjunctural."[11] The experience of black representation is quite instructive for my argument on how American Muslims should transcend a politics of representation that simply reverses negative depictions of Islam. In his influential essay, *New Ethnicities*, Hall describes two important phases in the history of black representation. The first phase was characterized by a desire of black artists to adopt the role of public relations officers rectifying stereotypes about their culture and creating what Hanif Kureishi calls "cheering fictions." The second phase was marked by a shift away from thinking that black culture is an essence that can be captured in an act of realistic depiction. Much like the label "black," the label "Muslim," to borrow Hall's words, is "essentially a politically and culturally constructed category, which cannot be grounded in a set of fixed trans-cultural or transcendental racial categories and which therefore has no guarantees in Nature."[12]

Like blacks before them, Muslims are confronting a phase of heavy stereotyping and political maneuvering that is dictated by geopolitical events outside of their control and by a lack of access to mainstream circles of representation in journalism, politics, and the art world. My argument is that unless they learn how to transcend this restrictive double burden of representation that limits the terms and extent of their public intervention, American Muslims will be stuck in a conventional culture of representation where their only mark is to create a sanitized and monolithic version of the "good Muslim." As mentioned earlier, the importance of this project of correcting negative depictions of Islam and Muslims cannot be slighted, but it is equally important for Muslims to publicly explore other dimensions of their lived experiences beyond a prescriptive agenda of cultural and religious politics.

Muslims in the Mountain West Project: An Exercise in Identity and Cultural Politics

In 2010, I began directing a research project that was broadly concerned with chronicling the undocumented history of Islam in the Mountain West and showcasing the complex diversity of Muslims in the region. *Muslims in the Mountain West*—a collaboration between the *Center of Media, Religion and Culture* and the *Center of Asian Studies* at the University of Colorado, Boulder, through a grant by the Social Science Research Council—also aimed at helping local media cover the Islam story beyond the crisis news angle of terrorism and security or as a foreign story forever tied to immigration and global geopolitics. Project researchers traveled to Wyoming, New Mexico, Idaho, Arizona, Montana, and various locations in Colorado to interview a variety of Muslims, curators of local historical societies, public intellectuals at local universities, and religion reporters at local newspapers, and they visited major Muslim landmarks in those states, including mosques and historic Muslim homes. And through a series of seminars, workshops, and media outreach initiatives, the project featured local and regional Muslim scholars, artists, activists, and scientists as integral threads in the cultural tapestry of the Rocky Mountains. This was meant to counter the prevailing politicized narrative of civilizational tensions and culturally irreducible differences between the West and the Muslim world. One of the main contributions of this project was a resource website that features video profiles of local Muslims, podcasts and photo slideshows about the history of Islam and Islamic landmarks in the region, and a documentary that tells fascinating stories of a variety of Rocky Mountain Muslims.

One of the biggest challenges in this project has been resisting the normative frames that strongly underlie much of the discussion of Islam in public discourse. We began our research and public outreach on this project as tensions flared up around the "Ground Zero mosque" controversy, and we quickly found ourselves compelled to address the very totalizing associations we sought so hard to disentangle. Our work was welcome and lauded in local media as a fresh departure from the negativity surrounding the story of Islam, but it was only discussed in close conjunction with the story of terrorism and security. Reporters, for example, suddenly noticed us around 9/11 anniversaries or to balance their reporting with a positive angle. Our events were generally better attended when our promotional flyers and brochures highlighted 9/11 as a critical context for the ongoing debate on Islam in American or in the West. Question-and-answer sessions at these events have been generally dominated by questions relating to terrorism, veiling, women's rights, sharia law, etc. The fact that 9/11 has become the only temporal frame through which Islam can be understood and against which Muslims can speak about their experiences and identities as Americans makes any attempt at refocusing this debate extremely difficult and at times simply impossible.

Against this formidable backdrop of "dangerous" Islam, it becomes inevitable that our counternarrative will be read as either defensive or unoriginal in the sense that it does not pose any threat and therefore is not relevant. Detailing the story of the first Muslim to have walked along the Colorado River in the 1530s, or of a Muslim camel herder hired by the US military to open up a camel route in the desert of Arizona in the 1850s, or of elite Christian families in the West holding mock dervish-style weddings in the 1800s, is quite interesting, and maybe exotic, to many people, but it does little to change the tune of the conversation about Islam. The point behind this historical detour is not to produce what Kureishi calls "cheering fictions" of Islam or to pretend terrorism is irrelevant. We simply hoped to decouple the label "Muslim" from the relentless political and cultural association that preconditions its appearance in public discourse. But the discursive and ahistorical brutality of these frames does at times dictate a position, or an imposed mandate, of promoting a less simplistic view of Islam and Muslim life, which might appear to some to be a public relations function. The dominant premise in these projects, however, is that only a foundational narrative is capable of reanchoring the debate on Islam.

Another important challenge we encountered in the course of this project was the primacy of the role of the "Muslim representative" who speaks on behalf of Islam and can only speak from his or her religious or ethnic background. This is consistent with the expectation arising from mainstream media coverage of Islam that has made Muslims visible exclusively around issues of religious tension, geopolitics, or security. Even when we tried to steer away from these frames, questions and feedback from the public frequently wondered how representative the "alternative" voices we featured are of mainstream ideas of Islam.

The fact that Muslims and their work should always be judged and compared against a normative framework of what constitutes real Islam is problematic because it reduces the label "Muslim" to an ontological essence that denies any individual agency or sees it only as a marginal reality. Artists or activists, for example, do what they do only from a religious conviction, even when their faith has little to do with their work. But their work is invoked in public discourse, as argued earlier, only in close conjunction with the ethnic and religious label of "Muslim." This creates a false expectation that Muslims always act as agents of their faith no matter what they do. This is not only the outcome of a myopic media coverage, but it is also aided by Muslims themselves who eagerly adopt this position and see themselves as the caretakers of Islam and their fellow Muslims. This collective identity politics, I argue, becomes easily packaged in terms of a relentless religious or ethnic essence that Muslims are poised to propagate. We purposefully invited writers and artists who challenge this expectation of religious or ethnic realism and prefer their work to be seen as individual articulations of difference from an ethnic, religious, gender, age, or sexuality perspective. Our premise here is that the Muslim experience is a function of lived culture and an act of self-definition in a larger society, not an essence in nature simply waiting for an accurate representation in the media.

By way of conclusion, I believe American Muslims, or Muslims anywhere for that matter, have to make this important shift of position if they wish to liberate themselves from this double burden of representation. There is still and will always be a need to intervene in hegemonic narratives of Islam, but Muslims, I contend, must rise above the realm of collective identity and religious politics as the only viable mechanism to reflect the "Muslim experience." An emerging generation of American Muslim storytellers have already made this transition, but their work is marginally featured in mainstream media and sometimes fiercely attacked by other Muslims who refute its critical stance and "blaring" individualism. But writing about the Muslim experience has to be complex and critical if we are to write it in the larger story of American diversity and cultural pluralism. The story of Muslims does not have to be always positive, culturally stable, collective, or always "right on." Both the media and the cultural production of Muslims can become a prime stage for this complex articulation. And Muslims themselves have to work harder at opening up the boundaries of the category "Muslim" away from its ghettoized religious connotation and its basic premise that if "good" Muslims can speak, things will be better. As Stuart Hall cautions in his reflections on black culture in the UK, "Films are not necessarily good because black people make them. They are not necessarily 'right-on' by virtue of the fact that they deal with the black experience. Once you enter the politics of the end of the essential black subject you are plunged headlong into the maelstrom of a continuously contingent, unguaranteed, political argument and debate: a critical politics, a politics of criticism. You can no longer conduct black politics through the strategy of a simple set of reversals, putting in the place of the bad old essential white subject, the new essentially good black subject."[13]

Nabil Echchaibi is Associate Professor of Media Studies and Associate Director of the Center for Media, Religion and Culture at the University of Colorado, Boulder. He is author of *Voicing Diasporas: Ethnic Radio in Paris and Berlin between Culture and Renewal* and coeditor of *International Blogging: Identity, Politics and Networked Publics.*

SEVEN

HOW DOES THE BRITISH PRESS REPRESENT BRITISH MUSLIMS? FRAMEWORKS OF REPORTING IN A BRITISH CONTEXT

Elizabeth Poole

PREFACE AND POSTSCRIPT

This chapter examines the representation of Muslims in Britain since 1994, over twenty years.[1] It highlights three main periods of coverage, pre-9/11, post-9/11, and post-7/7 (the July 7, 2005, terrorist attack in London), but since its initial drafting normative politics appears to have been turned on its head. Nationalist populist movements have gathered pace both across Europe and in the United States with, currently, one of the most visible political manifestations of this being Britain's decision to exit the EU following a referendum (popularly known as BREXIT, June 23, 2016). One explanation for this wave of nationalist populism is the felt effects of neoliberal globalization on those lower socioeconomic groups that feel disenfranchised in a postindustrial society. Populist groups have sought to capitalize on these circumstances by blaming immigration and immigrants for the demise of the nation and connecting the increase in immigration with a loss of sovereignty brought about through membership of the EU. Although it crossed political party lines, the Vote Leave campaign was dominated by Nigel Farage of UKIP, the UK Independence Party, a fiercely Euroskeptic, anti-immigration, right-wing, nationalist-populist party.

The Leave campaign quickly came to focus on immigration as its central rhetorical strategy, drawing on identity politics to win votes. With an

"insiders" and "outsiders" discourse, constructing clear boundaries between us and them (their main campaign slogan was "Take back control"),
the campaign found itself on common ground with much of the conservative press in Britain (which has a long history of xenophobic reporting)
and was able to dominate coverage. Research, only just emerging out of the
shadows of the referendum vote, shows that immigration was not only the
most prominent topic of media coverage in the conservative press, after the
economy, but across all national newspapers and on television, with the topic gaining further ground in the last few weeks of the campaign.[2]

Modood argues that the success of populist groups is based on oppositions along vertical (antielitism) and horizontal dimensions (Othering).[3]
The refugee crisis in Europe was used to attack liberal elites for their policies, which have led to a "dangerous excess" within, with refugees represented as sexual predators, security threats, and benefits spongers, common
themes in anti-Muslim discourse.[4] A stark example of the exploitation of
this identity politics was Nigel Farage's "Breaking point" poster, which featured a queue of Syrian (and therefore non-EU) refugees with the strapline
"We must take back control of our borders," perpetuating the myth of the
young male nonwhite (and here, Muslim) immigrant. While UKIP (during the campaign) was not explicit in the kind of anti-Islamism that has
been seen elsewhere in Europe and the United States, the adoption of this
binary approach created an atmosphere where racism and Islamophobia
was legitimized. An outcome of this divisionary politics was the murder of
Labour MP Jo Cox at her Northern constituency on June 16, 2016, by a far-
right Britain First supporter. As a response to this, a campaign group Hope
Not Hate—which promotes the creation of an inclusive Britain—was created in her memory. The election of Donald Trump as US president has also
led to some positive coverage of Muslims in the UK, often defending them
against explicit anti-Muslim racism. But the organization TellMamaUK,
which tracks hate speech and hate crimes in the UK, says that following the
BREXIT vote there was a marked increase in racist violence, including attacks on Muslims and mosques.

I write this on March 23, 2017, the day after what has been defined as an
Islamist-inspired terrorist attack on Westminster, London. While most of
the dailies' front pages focus on the victim of the attack, two tabloids and
the *Daily Mail* feature an image of the attacker, an image the outlets use to

link the attacker to Islamist terrorism. The response of Paul Nuttall, UKIP's current leader, is to say that "the Muslim community needs to root out this cancer within" (reported on the BBC). Nigel Farage has appeared on US television using the attack to bolster support for Trump's anti-Muslim policies.

We can trace a clear continuation across time in the themes and narratives informing the discourse about Muslims, with the main difference being in volume and strength. The tone of this discourse, however, is becoming more explicit, more negative, and more mainstream. This article provides the story of a long-standing framework of representation, which has contributed to a climate in which BREXIT became possible.

POLITICAL CONTEXT: PRE-9/11

Since the 1980s, neoliberal policies have accelerated economic globalization and resulted in the fragmentation and political uncertainties we are witnessing above. In the UK, this postmodern crisis of identity saw the reassertion of religious and national identities on the ground; the Rushdie affair is cited as an event that saw Muslims beginning to *mobilize around their religious identities*, for which their loyalty was questioned, furthering their politicization.[5] Also at the time, in a post–Cold War context, "Western" attention turned to various conflicts with neo-jihadist groups, which further contributed to a simplified representation of Muslims in the media.[6] So how did this play out in British press representation?[7]

Representation Pre 9/11

My first project examined coverage of British Muslims in two broadsheet newspapers (the *Times* / the *Guardian*) over a three-year period from 1994 to 1996 and subsequently in 1997 and 1999 to include two popular British tabloids (the *Sun* and the *Daily Mail*).[8] The first significant finding was that the focus on Islam was international; Islam was interpreted as largely foreign "Other." This is important given that the public's understanding of Muslims at home will intersect with representations of Muslims abroad (and the associations with barbarity, violence, and terrorism).[9] For example, over the three-year period, out of 6,507 articles about Islam (in the broadsheets), only 12.9 percent were about British Muslims or Muslims in Britain. Equally, in articles about British Muslims, world events were frequently cited, which had a homogenizing effect. This gap, however, consistently narrowed over the time period, particularly following the war in Iraq, and continues to do so according to subsequent research.[10]

Previous to 9/11, *Guardian* readers were presented with almost twice the amount of material as readers of the *Times*. The *Guardian*'s more extensive coverage of Islam has been based on a more accommodating approach to minority groups that allows space for alternative voices, while the more traditional values of the *Times* has meant that it is less likely to take an interest in items with less cultural proximity (in this case Islam) unless they have extreme news value. The events of September 11th and the war in Iraq allowed for the construction of Muslims (through a security framework) in a way that is more likely to be of interest to the conservative press.[11]

The themes that emerged from analyzing the coverage suggested to the public that: "Muslims involvement in deviant activities threatens security in the UK, Muslims are a threat to British mainstream values and thus provoke integrative concerns, there are inherent cultural differences between Muslims and the host community, which creates tensions in interpersonal relations, and Muslims are increasingly making their presence felt in the public sphere."[12]

These themes can be illustrated further by examining the dominant topics of coverage in relation to British Muslims. An analysis of topics allows for an identification of the type of material presented to the public on Islam and, therefore, the likely concerns and agenda of prevailing majority (ethnic) groups. Increased coverage then, implies that an issue has some salience or importance to the interests of powerful groups in a particular social context. What we can see is that a clear framework of news was developing in relation to British Muslims.

British Muslims were represented in relation to a relatively restricted range of issues, within which there were clear clusterings around certain topics that emerged as dominant (table 7.1). While there was a consistency in coverage from 1994 to 2003 with five topics dominating, it was also clear that the topics of politics, relationships, education, and crime, whose main focus are religious and cultural values (cultural clash) and which were at the forefront of coverage before 9/11, were overshadowed by coverage of terrorism and extremism after 9/11.

Table 7.1. Significant Topics on British Islam from 2003

1994–1996			2003		
Topic	*Total*	%	Topic	*Total*	%
Education	128	15.2	Terrorism	257	29.4
Relationships	60	7.1	War in Iraq	88	10
Fundamentalism	57	6.8	Politics	86	9.8
Politics	54	6.4	Education	71	8.1
Crime	43	5.1	Discrimination	34	3.9
Prince Charles	41	4.8	Crime	28	3.2
Media	41	4.8	Relationships	26	2.6
Belief	33	3.9	Race Relations	23	2.6
Freedom of Speech	28	3.3	Finance	18	2
Immigration	25	2.9	Relations to Christianity	17	1.9
Discrimination	21	2.5	Media	16	1.8
Total	**531**	**63.4**	**Total**	**641**	**73.2**
Total articles 1994–1996	**837**		**Total articles from 2003**	**875**	

This period of representation demonstrates how British Muslims were interpreted predominantly as a cultural threat prior to September 11th rather than a physical or security threat. It was foreign Muslims, exiled dissidents, who were categorized with the label "extremist" or "fundamentalist." Terrorism was perceived as mainly a foreign problem and social cohesion within could be maintained. A more detailed outline of these topics is provided in the following section, given the continuity in representation.

Post-9/11

September 11 is marked out as a significant event in the current political and historical context in that it signaled a discernible shift to a new politics categorized in specific "Western" countries by the "War on Terror." I would argue that this represents a continuation of processes that became more visible following 9/11. In other words, 9/11 has been mobilized politically, on both sides, to legitimize specific agendas, accelerating their course, with significantly negative effects. The consistency of the topics associated with

Islam, both British and global, found here is illustrative of a "framework of interpretation" that has dominated news reporting for several decades now. These findings have emerged out of four separate studies involving quantitative and qualitative analysis in 2001, 2003, 2007, 2008/9.[13]

The first point to note is the increase in volume in this period. In the aftermath of 9/11, between September 12, 2001, to October 25, 2001, the *Times* and the *Guardian* carried the equivalent of each paper's previous annual coverage.[14] There has been a year-by-year increase in coverage of *British* Muslims from 2000 to 2008 as they have become a suspect community, particularly since 7/7.[15] Coverage in the Conservative press overtook that of the Liberal as the framework of reporting shifted to focus on security issues (terrorism). The following section provides more details on how the dominant topics of coverage were represented.

"Islamic Terrorism"

The most significant shift in the coverage of British Muslims post-9/11 was in the association with terrorism. While this was clearly the prevailing image of global Islam prior to September 11, British Muslims were not given this label directly.[16] Rather, it was Muslims in Britain—exiles, dissidents, and asylum seekers—who were categorized as militant (and thus linked to terrorism). The shift occurred immediately following 9/11, and this has continued to be the dominant topic of coverage over the time period.[17]

Several common elements in these stories include:

Categorization. Various labels are used to categorize those engaged in what is predominantly defined as "Islamic terrorism." This might be "bombers," "violent Muslim fanatics," or "Islamic fundamentalists," among others.[18] Once people are labeled in this way, action against them does not have to be justified. This is not to legitimize acts of terror but to note the culturally embedded use of language and its implications for interpretation. The interchangeability of these categorizations and their use in the press makes one term easily replaceable with another, so that when "extremist" or "militant" is used, they are infused with ideas of terrorism.

Decontextualization. Rather than providing any historical or political context, the acts of terrorism are clearly linked to Islamic belief. The link between religion and violence was made frequently in coverage of the trial of the perpetrators of a terrorist attack on Glasgow Airport (2007). Here the perpetrators' Muslimness was emphasized; other motivations, if mentioned at all, were dismissed.

The Process of Othering. The process of Othering takes place by individualizing the perpetrator (and so divorcing him from the wider Muslim community and appeasing any accusations of racism) but then linking him to "radicals" outside the UK who have "brainwashed" the individual. Thus a link is made to Islamic ideology, which is given as the driving force, but it is also Othered by being located outside the UK. There are two significant processes here: characterization, that of the naïve individual who is susceptible to indoctrination, and technology, which is marked out as central to the process of radicalization in terms of "internet jihad" (*Times*, October 16, 2008, 3).[19]

This process was explicit in the reporting on Nick Reilly, a Muslim convert with Asperger's syndrome (and so, it was suggested, vulnerable to conditioning and conversion), who tried to detonate a bomb in a restaurant, but instead locked himself in the bathroom, where the first bomb exploded. He was subsequently arrested. In this case, Reilly was represented as a criminal (e.g., through mug shots) but his networks and contacts outside the UK were emphasized. It was these that had "groomed" him with their "extreme religious and murderous ideology" (*Times*, October 10, 2008, 22–23).[20] Thus the connection was made to Islam, but the responsibility was placed outside the UK. Adopted in articles in both the *Sun* and the *Times*, this strategy was evident in the opening sentence of the latter: "A vulnerable Muslim convert was persuaded online by shadowy Pakistan-based extremists into trying to carry out a suicide bomb attack on a busy restaurant" (*Times*, October 10, 2008, p. 22–23).[21]

In a supporting article, the *Times*'s crime and security editor concluded that Reilly had been "radicalized from afar" and quoted the "respected Jamestown Foundation" arguing that the Internet had "become the easiest and safest way . . . to reach young militants, who likely lack training, and steer them under al-Qaeda's general command."[22]

There are, of course, articles on terrorism that offer an alternative viewpoint, for example, criticism of counterterrorism measures such as the controversial 2005 control orders that placed significant restrictions on terrorist suspects. But the volume of negative coverage clearly outweighs this coun-terdiscourse. The lack of commentary around these stories further demon-strates a consensus of opinion.

Conflict/Extremism

There is, of course, an overlap between all the topics I'm discussing here, but in this category I have included articles that are not explicitly labeled as terrorist. Conflict stories tend to feature Britons caught up in world con-flict zones. "Extremism" relates to activities that may previously have been labeled "fundamentalism" but do not explicitly refer to terrorism. This topic is encapsulated by (predominantly tabloid) press coverage of "preachers of hate." The term "preachers of hate" has been coined by the tabloid press to describe Muslim clerics (located in the UK) who preach an anti-Western message. Rarely, the term will be applied to someone outside Islam if they are deemed "extreme" enough. For example, it has been used to describe Fred Phelps, the leader of the Westboro Baptist Church, an extreme Ameri-can Christian group. The term was not applied to Geert Wilders, the anti-Islamic Dutch MP, who could be accused of "hate speech."

A useful example is the *Sun*'s obsessive pursuit of Omar Bakri Moham-med and Abu Hamza, frequently characterized as "Evil Hook."[23] This and other articles referred to specific examples of hate speech and associations with terror, and yet also demonstrated the individual's perfidiousness. For example, Omar Bakri Muhammad is a well-known and caricatured Islamist leader who was born in Syria but lived in London from 1986 to 2005 (he is now banned from the UK). He was responsible for the development of sev-eral Islamist organizations in the UK and was used by the media for easy, sensational quotes. In espousing anti-Western ideas, however, he was also a target. Before 9/11, Bakri Mohammed was dismissed as a buffoon, but in post-7/7 Britain, his outpourings became particularly unpalatable. The *Sun* has published stories featuring his divorce and new young wife, his pole dancer daughter, and ex-wife's fraud to demonstrate his hypocrisy.

These articles also operate as a positive representation of the in group, the tolerance of the British compared to "their" intolerance: "People in this country do all they can to understand the Muslim way of life,"[24] yet "they" object to the most innocuous things such as the television entertainment program *The X Factor*.[25] Each recurring story confirms the pattern of behavior. The simplistic characterization makes the clerics easy to dismiss (hate and blame) without any further contextual information. There is no evidence of counterdiscourse. An anti-immigrationist discourse is also evident, particular in relation to the exploitation of the welfare system. Immigrants, more generally, have become scapegoats for all the uncertainties of living in a globalized world.

Prior to 9/11, coverage of British Muslims caught up in world conflict zones was limited, but the idea that British Muslims were being radicalized abroad gathered pace and has subsequently led to more extensive reporting. The Iraq War was also a major topic of coverage in relation to British Muslims in 2003 as they were invited to comment on events and their reactions and protests were reported on. Positive articles sympathized with Muslims' perspectives and had a certain political expediency as they were used to criticize government policy (mainly in the *Guardian*). Coverage, however, tended to assume one Muslim perspective as both interested in and opposed to the war.

Coverage of conflict after 9/11 has mainly focused on ongoing events in Iraq and Afghanistan and subsequently the fallout of the Arab Spring. These stories often construct Muslims, given their distance from the UK, as with the terrorist Other (or as victims; currently as refugees). Distant conflict zones allow for the construction of Muslims as bogeymen, as in the example of the Taliban. One such story was that of the death of aid worker Gayle Williams, shot in Afghanistan by the Taliban in October 2008. Here, the Taliban are constructed in such a way (as irrational but purposeful, driven by irrational ideology, cowardly murderers) that there is little need to justify action against them.

It is not the aim of this research to try and measure the accuracy of these reports but to suggest that the excessive focus on extremism in relation to Islam, while paying little attention to the variety of Muslim life, homogenizes and presents to the general public a skewed idea of what Islam is.

Cultural Values/Differences

This theme, which suggests that Muslims have inherently different cultural and religious values that conflict with "British values" (a construction) dominates the coverage of British Muslims and runs through a variety of popular topics, such as education, relationships, legal issues, gender issues, religious practice, criminality, and political values. This has been a dominant topic of coverage throughout the time period.

While there has been a shift in the types of stories used to express this since the late 1990s, there has been little change in the message that within a binary exclusive relationship "we," the British, have been too tolerant. This tolerance has been abused by "them" as they seek to impose "their" way of life on "us." Many of these articles therefore concentrate on the restrictive censorious "nature" of Islam in contrast to liberal Britain. Examples of this include coverage of the veil, honor killings, conversion, Muslim protest, Muslim separatism, immigration, censorship versus freedom of speech. Since 9/11 these articles have increasingly highlighted the "persecution" of Christians and focused on the increasing "Islamification" of the UK made possible by weak government. This was a dominant theme in the reporting on Geert Wilders, a Dutch MP for the Party for Freedom (PVV), who has been vocal in highlighting "Islamification." When invited to a screening of *Fitna*, his anti-Islamic film, in the House of Lords, Wilders was refused entry to Britain on public order grounds. Aware that he would be turned back at the airport, Wilders flew to London, thus achieving a huge publicity coup. Rather than choosing to protect a minority group from attack, media coverage focused on the juxtaposition of freedom of speech (constructed as a liberal Western value) versus censorship (here a product of Islam's prohibitionist nature). The government was presented as undermining "British values" by tolerating "preachers of hate" while banning Wilders. Appeasement and double standards were key themes.

I have obviously simplified here due to the need to summarize the main findings of longitudinal research, thus reducing the nuances in coverage and differences between media forms and outlets to a generalized message. For example, outlets such as the *Guardian*, *Channel 4*, and the *BBC* regularly feature alternative counterdiscourse that runs against the dominant forms of representation. Television coverage appears to be more diverse than the press because of the wider variety of genres featured. There are indications from analysis of a regional paper, the *Yorkshire Evening Post*, that the local press has a different set of news values that leads to more inclusivity. This is evident in its coverage of community relations and interfaith activities but also in reports, rare elsewhere, that depict Muslims as ordinary everyday community members. Hence coverage should not be taken for granted. Positive coverage often occurs in unexpected places. As societies diversify and Muslims gain a greater presence in the public sphere, so coverage will evolve.

WHAT CAN PRACTITIONERS LEARN FROM THIS?

- Careful use of terminology. Think about the use of categorization, characterization, and agency when composing reports.
- Reflect the diversity, complexity, and richness of Muslim populations, experience, and life.
- Take time to understand complex geohistorical political processes that have resulted in increased diversity, immigration, and globalization. This context should be available to audiences, and expanding digital forms provide a resource to allow for this.
- Avoid simplifications, generalizations, and reverting to stereotypical binaries.
- Avoid using the religious identifier "Muslim" if it is inappropriate.
- Try to work outside the established framework of reporting, avoiding culturally embedded assumptions. Looking to alternative sources supports this approach.

WHAT CAN WE LEARN FROM MEDIA PRODUCERS?

Interviews with producers working in minority and mainstream media in the UK can offer further insights into the structural and professional context that impacts coverage of diversity issues.[26] The Muslim media producers we interviewed demonstrated a professional, critical, and intelligent journalistic approach. Their aim was to have a positive impact that countered negative media coverage and provided a more nuanced understanding of diversity issues, which reflected their own acute understanding of these. Their organizations were not sectarian, and they were keen to differentiate themselves from "religious" media that might seek to propagate Islam. The producers were critical of mainstream media and, in particular, the limited and extreme sources used to represent Muslim opinion. Cited as generally missing in coverage were the spiritual aspects of Islam, its diversity, achievements, and contributions to civilization, attacks on Muslims, depth, detail, and Muslim voices.

It was the critical awareness that these journalists had of changes in recent decades—global geopolitics and migration, which had led to social fracture and religious diversity—which they felt did not frame the debates about Muslims and related issues in the mainstream media. The British (tabloid) press came in for particular criticism. Some organizations such as the *Guardian* were praised for their coverage, as was Britain in general, which was felt to be a generally positive and diverse cultural and social environment, particularly in comparison to the rest of Europe.

The producers commented on the polarizing effect of mainstream coverage and suggested that Muslim media could provide an outlet for this frustration. It could offer a voice to excluded opinions and also provide a range of sources for mainstream media. Unfortunately, the interviews with mainstream media (non-Muslim) producers showed that it has not yet realized this potential except in the case of some liberal outlets. Overall the participants felt that negative coverage had led to Muslims being intensely skeptical toward mainstream media and a loss of credibility, even for those with a reputation for balance such as the BBC.

Those producers of a Muslim background working in mainstream media experienced tension in making production decisions and covering Muslim stories. They have to struggle with the "burden of responsibility," the tension between not wanting to be pigeonholed and taking the opportunity to provide positive images to counter the negative. While most recognized the value of their Muslim identity for providing understanding in relation to Muslim issues and having access to and engaging with diverse communities, they also wanted to be given the opportunity to write about a wider range of topics.

These producers also felt that mainstream newsrooms, besides tokenistic approaches to meeting quotas through the use of ethnic minority presenters, still appear to be largely white, middle class, and male. Producers were aware of the production pressures and other aspects of the industry, for example commercial imperatives, that often resulted in reverting to type, but they felt that complexity could be represented within these constraints.

WHAT CAN WE LEARN FROM CONSUMERS?

In addition to producer interviews, the project included focus groups and a survey with both Muslim (50) and non-Muslim (110) consumers. Overwhelmingly, the research found that people thought the media was biased against Muslims. For most Muslims this led them to disregard particular products. For some, skepticism toward the media was so strong that all organizations were viewed with suspicion. In general, though, among Muslims and non-Muslims, mainstream media was still the preferred source for news. For most people this was the BBC, including the World Service, closely followed by Al-Jazeera as an alternative when mainstream media was seen to be lacking. Traditional (television) viewing habits are preferred, supported by new (online) content and sources. This shows how people will remain with mainstream media if they are provided with the quality and diversity they expect, but the rise of Al-Jazeera and skepticism toward the BBC demonstrate the fragility of this relationship if organizations choose to ignore the increasing diversity and global reality of demographics and their associated media consumption practices. Young Muslims' media practices, in particular, mirrored that of their non-Muslim peers. Mainstream media should seek to be inclusive and would be foolish to lose this audience due to issues of trust.

Of course, religious identity is not always at the forefront of decision making in relation to media consumption. People demonstrated selectivity in their approach to media use, deriving pleasure from some aspects of mainstream media (for example fashion) while avoiding coverage of diversity issues in some publications.

Most Muslims, in this sample, supported multiculturalism, believed that it worked well in Britain, and that living in mixed societies brings positive benefits. They assertively claimed their Britishness despite their awareness of negative discourses in the UK context. But they also believed that media coverage has a negative impact on ideas about Muslims among non-Muslims, and this makes them more reluctant to mix. In this way the media does therefore contribute to divisions in society. Evidence from a monocultural (non-Muslim) focus group where participants conflated coverage with reality indicates this. This should be recognized, and organizations should take some responsibility for their coverage and its impact.

Suggestions for Change

- There should be greater interaction between minority and mainstream media. This should be used a source for mainstream media to share a more nuanced history of relations between Islam and the West.
- Research such as this should feed into journalism education.
- There should be clear and formal policies on diversity and editorial policy. Evidence from broadcasting shows that these can have a positive impact. While informal arrangements may work at small or progressive organizations, a more rigorous approach demonstrated by the regulation of broadcasting could also have a positive impact on other organizations. Clear communication of these policies to staff is needed.
- Employers should recognize both the value and importance of employing a wider diversity of people in their workplace.
- Editors should use their journalists as a resource for greater understanding but should not always foreground their religious or ethnic identity.
- There should be further regulation of the industry to instill ethical responsibility.

Conclusion

A loss of "Britishness" (due to globalization) has been blamed on the foreigner within and has led to a reassertion of "British values," which exclude Muslims who have invested in religious identity as a source of pride. This has been systematically interpreted as a threat to cohesion with forced segregation (through institutional racism and industrial decline) reformulated as separatism.[27] The response among some groups is evident in public and press discourse as they seek to establish hegemony. In a speech to a Munich Security Conference, almost ten years after 9/11, then prime minister David Cameron blamed multiculturalism for Islamic extremism (due to minority separatism) and set out a test for "extremism." In a postterrorist environment, support for multiculturalism has given way to the politics of community cohesion and integration (assimilation), a legacy of the previous Labour government. In this context, media practitioners have a responsibility to engage in ethical journalism for the sake of healthy community relations.

Elizabeth Poole has published widely in the area of the representation and reception of Muslims in the news. She is author of *Reporting Islam: Media Representations of British Muslims, Muslims and the News Media* and coauthor of *Media Portrayals of Religion and the Secular Sacred*.

EIGHT

HOW TO WRITE ABOUT MUSLIMS

Sobia Ali-Faisal and Krista Riley

RULE #1: DON'T ASSUME THAT MUSLIM WOMEN NEED TO BE SAVED, OR THAT YOU KNOW HOW TO SAVE THEM

More specifically, avoid assuming that all Muslim women are somehow oppressed at the hands of their fellow Muslims. The Muslim community is just as diverse as any other. (This is an important point. You'll notice it will come up again and again.) By generalizing in such a way, you malign the entire community, including women. This is offensive to the many women who are treated with respect and equality by their fellow Muslims, including Muslim men. This assumption also ignores the forms of oppression that Muslim women may be facing from outside the Muslim community, such as racism and Islamophobia (or even war and occupation, in cases like Iraq and Afghanistan), which for some women can be at least as disastrous as anything they experience in their Muslim community.

Don't assume that Muslim women can't take care of themselves. This is very patronizing. Muslim women have agency, and a great deal of it. Throughout history, and today, Muslim women have been taking on various leadership roles. In situations where women are being oppressed, they are often resisting in ways the media doesn't always think about. Additionally, most Muslim countries have Muslim women's organizations that are working hard to support themselves and other women.

Don't automatically assume that what you're going to do for Muslim women is going to be helpful. The assumption is that you know better than they do what's good for them. It also suggests that you are actually in a position to help them, which might not be true.

RULE #2: RATHER THAN ASSUMING YOU KNOW WHAT MUSLIM WOMEN'S LIVES ARE LIKE, TRY ASKING THEM

Too often, writers write about Muslim women without ever trying to find out what Muslim women's lives are like from their own perspective. This is poor research and feeds into the problematic assumptions discussed in Rule #1. Do your homework and try hard to connect to the specific women you are writing about. Even if you are writing about women in another country, try to connect to women's organizations in that country. At the very least, try to connect to women from that country who are living in your own community.

RULE #3: DON'T ASSUME THAT MUSLIM MEN ARE INHERENTLY VIOLENT OR TERRORIST OR OPPRESSING WOMEN

In other words, make sure to avoid writing as if any criminal or violent act a Muslim man commits, regardless of reason or context, is somehow a part of his nature as a Muslim man. Remember that when a non-Muslim man, specifically a white non-Muslim man, engages in the exact same criminal activity or commits the exact same act of violence there is no assumption that his behavior is caused by his being white or his religion. The same goes for Muslim men. The Muslim men who do engage in such behaviors do so for a variety of reasons that include economic, historical, political, social, etc., just like men who are not Muslim. Muslim men don't have some "violence gene." Muslim men are extremely diverse in every way possible, and assuming they're all violent maligns all Muslim men. This is offensive to the many Muslim men who would never engage in violence, terrorism, or criminal activity.

Avoid assuming that context does not matter or that it does not affect anyone's actions. When some Muslim men do engage in violence or terrorism, they do not do so in a vacuum. They do so because of their context; perhaps for them it's a means of getting out of poverty, a response to war or external threat, or a reaction to oppression. Recognizing the context within which these acts occur does not excuse them, but it highlights the reality and the truth that those Muslim men who do such things do not do them "just for fun" or for no reason at all. It highlights the reality that Muslim men do not, once again, have a "violence gene." Context is extremely important to take into account. Extremely.

Avoid suggesting that Muslim men have a monopoly on oppressing women. Virtually every society in the world, including those in North America, is patriarchal; men have more power than women. Muslim societies and communities are no exception. Muslim men are no different than other men when it comes to treatment of women: some treat women well, others not so much. Again, remember, Muslim men are extremely diverse. Don't make generalizations about how all Muslim men treat all Muslim women. Once again, doing so maligns all Muslim men and is offensive to all the Muslim men who treat women with respect.

Rule #4: Be Careful of Who You Talk to Regarding Islam and/or Muslims

Don't assume, just because someone is Muslim, that all Muslims will agree with that person or that that person represents all Muslims. For example, Muslims who have made a career out of calling other Muslims Islamists, and who base their credibility on the number of other Muslims who don't like them, are probably not a good source of information. Generally, people who work within a framework that takes Islam and Muslims into account in a respectful way and who recognize and respect the diversity of beliefs among Muslims and within Islam, as opposed to those who always bash Islam and Muslims, are more likely to understand the Muslim community. Again, this goes back to a point made earlier about not making generalizations about Muslims. If the Muslims you're speaking with start making sweeping generalizations about all Muslims, then it may be good sign that they probably lack understanding of the Muslim community.

If you're looking for information on Islam and Muslims, books and articles by the following people might be of interest: Jasmin Zine, Asifa Quraishi, Amina Wadud, Ayesha Chaudhry, Su'ad Abdul Khabeer, Kecia Ali, Omid Safi, Sana Saeed, and Shireen Ahmed. (Note that neither we nor *Muslimah Media Watch* necessarily endorse everything that any of these people say.)

RULE #5: UNDERSTAND THAT MUSLIMS ARE JUST LIKE ANYONE ELSE IN TERMS OF THEIR BELIEF SYSTEMS—NOT EVERYTHING A MUSLIM DOES HAS TO DO WITH ISLAM

Although Islam may play an important role in the lives of many Muslims, this does not mean that every action a Muslim takes, good or bad, is related to her or his religion. Believing that everything a Muslim does must be related to Islam is the same as believing that everything Christians, Jews, Hindus, or Sikhs do is related to their religions. As irrational and nonsensical as this seems for these religious groups, it should seem equally as nonsensical to apply this belief to Muslims. The ways Muslims behave, just like the ways all people behave, are influenced by the many experiences in our lives, only one of which is religion. To assume that a Muslim's behavior is based on religion alone is to assume that Muslims live in a vacuum that is devoid of culture, economy, patriarchy, social problems, health issues, and so on.

RULE #6: UNDERSTAND THAT THERE IS NO SUCH THING AS A "MUSLIM CULTURE"—MUSLIMS COME FROM A VARIETY OF CULTURES, AND CULTURE IS DYNAMIC

Muslim culture does not exist. There is no one region of the world from which Muslims hail. Don't take our word for it. Ask any researcher in cross-cultural studies, and they will tell you that a singular Muslim culture does not exist.

Muslims come from a variety of different cultures, and culture is a dynamic phenomenon. Every culture is constantly changing. Hence, the cultures from which Muslims originate are also changing. What may have happened in a culture fifty years ago may not necessarily happen today. Moreover, cultures are diverse, and people within them don't all do exactly the same things. Just as non-Muslim North Americans are not drones acting in ways dictated to them by their culture, similarly Muslims, in North America and abroad, do not mindlessly follow their respective cultures. Don't create a dichotomy between "Muslim" and "Western" (or "Canadian," "American," "European," etc.)

For example, "American women" and "Muslim women" are often talked about as if they're mutually exclusive categories. Perhaps it seems obvious that, in such cases, we should be understanding this as "[non-Muslim]

American women" and "[non-American] Muslim women," but language is important, and it's a serious problem if the many women who identify both as American and as Muslim end up excluded from these discussions. For non-Muslim Americans (or for non-American Muslims), it could reinforce the idea of "American" identity as inherently non-Muslim and of "Muslim" identity as inherently foreign to the United States.

There are a lot of Muslims who also identify as Western, Canadian, American, and so on. Talking about Westerners and Muslims as if the categories are mutually exclusive reinforces the idea of an irreconcilable divide between Islam and the West and erases the identities of the many Muslims who feel connected to both categories.

RULE #7: "MUSLIM ISSUES" ARE NOT ALWAYS WHAT YOU THINK

Over the past few years, many Muslims have spoken out about the need to support the Black Lives Matter movement, sometimes with non-Black Muslims taking the spotlight in order to point to a need for alliances between Muslim communities and Black communities. After the Pulse nightclub shooting in 2016, where fifty people were murdered by a Muslim man at a gay nightclub in Orlando, there were several news stories and statements about Muslim and LGBT communities standing together against violence.

These stories seem like positive pieces of good news until we look at some of the language. In many of these cases, alliances between Muslim and LGBT communities, or between Muslim and Black communities, are discussed as if the categories are mutually exclusive. "Muslim issues" and "queer issues" are framed as separate, as are "Muslim issues" and "Black issues," so these moments of coming together are seen as rare. While at times this might be the case at the level of leadership of some of the communities involved, this construction erases the fact that many Muslims *are* queer, or Black, or both (and we can add other categories here too). In fact, most estimates suggest that Black Muslims are the largest group of Muslims in the United States, even though Muslims tend to be portrayed as mainly Arab or South Asian. Anti-Black racism and homophobia are forms of oppression that touch many Muslims directly; these aren't only issues of alliance across different Muslim communities but are also issues that Muslims face.

In other words, the realm of "Muslim issues" encompasses more than France's laws about headscarves or the many iterations of the US government's "Muslim ban." Homophobia and anti-Black racism *are* Muslim issues. Some journalists have done an excellent job of highlighting Black Muslim voices when it comes to these intersections, and many articles were published after the Orlando massacre highlighting the voices of queer Muslims. Still, there remains much work to be done.

RULE #8: TONE IT DOWN!
BE MINDFUL OF THE LANGUAGE YOU USE

Language is a powerful tool that can shape people's perceptions and can have far-reaching implications for the way people are seen. When every act of domestic violence committed by a Muslim is called an "honor killing," and every other violent act seen as "terrorism," without any attention to context, Muslims get painted as uniquely violent, with labels that are rarely applied to most non-Muslims who commit similar acts. Terms like these can easily be used to portray all Muslims (and the cultures that Muslims are assumed to come from) as violent, scary, oppressed, dangerous, and so on. It's useful for fear mongering but often antithetical to responsible journalism.

Similarly, be careful of words like "shariah," "jihad," and "fatwa," the meanings of which are much more complex than is usually acknowledged. "Sharia" encompasses a broad legal system the human interpretations of which are understood to be diverse and imperfect; "jihad" refers to internal spiritual struggles as well as external wars; a "fatwa" is a religious decision on virtually any topic and only rarely refers to a death threat. So be sure to fully and properly understand the words before you use them. You may end up realizing that the word you thought was appropriate doesn't make any sense in the context you wanted to use it. (Some of the religious scholars we mentioned in Rule #4 might be able to help you out with the meanings of some of these words.)

Be careful also of phrases like "Islam says," which often give narrow interpretations that don't express the breadth of meanings that Islam can have.

RULE #9: STOP TRYING TO LABEL AND CATEGORIZE MUSLIMS

Muslims decide for themselves how to identify, so we don't need others to do so for us. Terms like "moderate" are often not ones that Muslims have chosen or defined. These are meaningless to most Muslims. What does "moderate" mean? Who decides how a "moderate" Muslim acts, worships, behaves, etc.? What is the difference between a "moderate Muslim" and one who is not moderate? These questions cannot be answered because the term "moderate" is meaningless.

Allow Muslims to identify themselves however they choose without imposing your own views, values, or terms on them. Don't decide who is a "good" Muslim, or who is a "bad" Muslim either. Many make the mistake of assuming that those Muslims who are not religious, traditional, or conservative are somehow the "good" (safe, unthreatening) ones while those who are religious, traditional, or conservative are the "bad" (violent, unpredictable) ones. This is problematic because it demonizes the many religious or conservative Muslims for no reason other than their interpretation of their religion while assuming lack of religiousness or conservatism to be ideal.

Similarly, don't assume religiosity, including conservative religiosity, to be an extremist position. Religiosity does not equal extremism. As we've mentioned numerous times already, Muslims are diverse. Similarly, Islam is diverse. There is no one way to be religious. An individual can be religious in a variety of ways. Only a small minority of those who are religious may be extremist.

RULE #10: TAKE RESPONSIBILITY FOR THE CONSEQUENCES OF YOUR WRITING

If you do decide to write in ways that seem to generalize, patronize, insult, or demonize a whole group of people, then take responsibility for your words and realize that people will be offended and upset. Do not be surprised when people feel insulted, demonized, or belittled by your words. And do not be surprised when they critique it on blogs or write seething letters to the editor.

RULE #11: LEAVE THE HEADSCARF ALONE

The headscarf is really not the most important issue in the lives of most Muslim women. And most Muslim women would really appreciate it if the media would figure this out soon. There is almost nothing new that could possibly be said about the headscarf, and we are getting very bored.

Muslim women wear (or don't wear) the headscarf for a variety of reasons. Many Muslim women who wear the headscarf believe it is their religious obligation, while others wear it to increase their spirituality, or as an expression of their modesty, or for political reasons, or because of cultural or family expectations; others may wear it for all or none of the above reasons. Many Muslim also choose not to wear the hijab because they feel it is not a religious obligation, or because they live in a context where they feel uncomfortable wearing it. Whatever their beliefs may be, for most Muslim women the headscarf is a personal and private choice, a choice they have the right and ability to make. They might even change their mind from time to time. Assuming that the headscarf is somehow inherently problematic undermines the agency of the women who have chosen to either wear or not wear the headscarf.

Even for women who are in situations where headscarves are imposed, they are probably having lots of other things imposed on them too. The obsessive and often exclusive focus on the scarf is still reductive and misses the point.

Really, it's getting old. Give it a rest.

RULE #12: NEVER GO "BEHIND THE VEIL"

We know; we just told you to stop thinking about the headscarf. So what better way to overcome that focus than to go "behind" it, right? Or some other combination of the formula "behind/beneath/under/beyond" + "the" + "veil/hijab/burka/niqab" for your headline? That formula is used in the headlines for an absurd number of articles on Muslims.

Here's why it's a bad idea:

This kind of headline is horribly uncreative and nauseatingly repetitive. Even if this were the most brilliant, witty headline ever (which it isn't; see below for why), it has been done so many times that we can't imagine why no one has put a stop to it yet. To illustrate just how overdone this title is, a Google search of "behind the veil" (in quotes) gives about 1,290,000 results, including articles and books on women in Iran, "Western" journalists' encounters with "women in conservative Islamic societies," representations of Muslim women in Indian writings, an Australian woman's experiences as a nurse in Saudi Arabia, prostitution in Iran, HIV/AIDS in Muslim countries, and reports from several sources on women in Afghanistan. The point is, it's been done, ad nauseam, especially (but not exclusively) with regard to Muslim women, and "behind the veil" as a name is just plain lazy. Maybe that sounds harsh, but this frustration comes from having seen titles like this time and time again, and the implication that the only reason to pay attention to Muslim women is in order to de-veil them.

It emphasizes the veil as a symbol of Otherness and its wearers as inherently different from the writer (as well as the writer's imagined audience, which is presumed to be unveiled). It also tells women who wear various forms of veils that they are inherently difficult, if not impossible, to understand and that their veil is the main factor in any of their interactions with the nonveiled public.

It delegitimizes the role of the veil as part of a woman's experience. By assuming that we have to go "beyond" the veil in order to truly know someone, we are assuming that the veil exists only as a barrier to understanding a person's identity, rather than being a part of her identity that she is choosing to express. This isn't to say that the veil is the be-all-and-end-all of a person's identity, of course, but the assumption that we cannot properly know someone unless she is unveiled denies the possibility that understanding her relationship to the veil may actually be part of the process of knowing her.

Going behind the veil is invasive. Head or face coverings are often worn specifically to cover a part of the body that the wearers are choosing to keep out of the public eye. Claiming this right to go under the veil violates the decision that the wearer has made about which parts of her body are up for public viewing. We wouldn't try to write an in-depth portrayal of someone entitled "behind the shirt" or "beneath the pants." Let's try to stay away from symbolic undressing altogether, okay?

There really isn't anything all that interesting behind the veil anyway. You really want to know what's behind it? Often there's hair, there's usually a head, and occasionally a face. It's not that exciting. For those who were hoping that the veil was there to conceal superhuman beauty, Medusa-like snake hair, or secret alien antennae, we're sorry to disappoint.

This chapter draws from a similar piece of writing the authors produced for *Muslimah Media Watch*.

Sobia Ali-Faisal holds a PhD in applied social psychology from the University of Windsor, where she researched the sexual health of young Muslim adults living in Canada and the United States. She is founder of the nonprofit Sah'ha: Muslim Sexual Health Network and a contributor to *Muslimah Media Watch* (www.muslimahmediawatch.org), a blog examining representations of Muslim women in media and popular culture.

Krista Riley is Editor-in-Chief of *Muslimah Media Watch* (www.muslimahmediawatch.org), a blog that looks at representations of Muslim women in media and popular culture. She holds a PhD in communication studies from Concordia University in Montreal, where her research focused on Muslim feminist blogs as spaces of religious interpretation.

NINE

A JOURNALIST REFLECTS ON COVERING MUSLIM COMMUNITIES

Robert King

THE QUESTION OF WHAT A journalist should know about "representing" Muslims and Islam is an interesting one, and a bit uncomfortable. As journalists, we are supposed to present stories and people as we find them. The notion that we would "represent" any group or faith carries an element of public relations to it that makes us squirm. We are not spokespersons for our subjects. We are supposed to represent only the people who consume our work: readers, viewers, or listeners. Sometimes our work benefits our subjects' cause, sometimes it hurts them, but our duty is only to the truth, as best as a fallible reporter with a deadline can discern it. Yet it's true that what we write and report reflects our subjects to the world, sometimes positively, sometimes in an unflattering light. Whatever it does, we want to it to be as close to the truth as we can get it. But there are obstacles in our way.

First, we are drawn magnetically to certain stories and narratives that grow around the subjects and people we cover. They tug at us like the current in a river, drawing us to the easy stories, ones that follow the prevailing winds of conventional wisdom, or sometimes just the loudest voices. This is where journalists can fail both our audience and a Muslim population that faces enough challenges without the media's help. When we describe people and ideas to the world, we do make a representation of them. We write their history, or at least the early drafts.

We serve them up for dissection and discussion. It is a high responsibility, and it is incredibly important that we do it fairly and without varnish.

Like most American journalists, my reporting on Muslims was limited before 9/11. Afterward, we couldn't write enough. We covered the initial stories about anti-Muslim reaction to the attacks: shots fired at mosques, women in hijab being harassed, and the like. We reported how American Muslims were horrified by the attacks, how they explained that theirs was a religion of peace. But then we were left to square that with the fanatical religious devotion of the 9/11 attackers, the relatively small portion of the Muslim world that cheered their "success," and the ongoing reality of suicide bombers shouting "God is great!" as they blew up street markets in Baghdad. Closer to home, the feds were raiding Muslim charities and shutting some of them down while making arrests in others. Taking hold was the notion that not only were there potential sleeper cells of Muslim terrorists among us, but that American Muslims might be helping support the cause. It created a Red Scare effect we still haven't quite shaken. All this led to more questions, more understanding, and more reporting. It still does. This is why what you're doing is important. But how do you do it responsibly?

Remember the Fundamentals

The fundamentals of our trade are our best guide in reporting on Muslims and Islam. Most journalists reporting about Muslims will be encountering a faith that's not their own and, in the case of immigrant Muslims, people who speak a different language and who have different customs. But the essentials of reporting never change. You may begin your reporting with a thesis but you have to go in with an open mind. Ask plenty of questions of your subjects.

If you are still struggling to understand an answer, keep asking until you figure it out. The truism applies here that it's better to annoy your sources with questions than to err in your final report. Better yet, be skeptical. Be a devil's advocate. Don't be afraid to ask the questions about the notions held by your Islamophobic uncle, the ones you begin with the phrase, "What about the people who say all Muslims are . . ." In a decade of interviewing Muslims, I've never had anyone object to such questions. Sometimes these produce the best quotes with the greatest insight. Enjoy the license that comes with being a journalist that allows you to ask awkward questions.

Know Your Subject

Knowing your subjects is always important. It's especially helpful in covering Muslim communities and writing about Islam. Read the Qur'an, or at least an English version of it. It's not that long. The Islamaphobes in the world love to ask, "Have you ever read the Qur'an?" Being able to say "Yes" is quite satisfying and useful. But don't stop there. Read about the history of Islam, and the peoples who practice it. You don't have to park yourself in a library to do this.

Just pay attention to what better, more experienced journalists—Thomas Friedman is one of my favorites—are already writing about Muslims, Islam, and the "Muslim world." Pay special attention to his reporting about the Israel-Palestinian conflict. This issue resonates with Muslims around the world. If at first you don't grasp the history, keep reading. Listen to Muslims talk about their own history of the faith. Learn how the Muslim community in your city came to be. Generalization alert here: Most Muslims love to talk about such things.

Be a Skeptic

Know that there is a world of misinformation about what Muslims believe, what the Qur'an says, and what Muslim American institutions are all about. View with the greatest caution and skepticism the library of books, the cache of "antiterrorism" websites, and assorted "newsletters" that purport to know of hidden conspiracies within Muslim institutions and among individuals. At times, such sources are about as reliable as the tales of the Old West written by easterners who'd never been west of the Mississippi. There are good number of "experts" peddling books about the threat of "Islamofascism" and going on speaking tours to discuss these topics (while selling their books). For many of these people, their only credentials are that they are speakers and authors. Don't anoint someone in your story an "expert" unless he or she has some real credentials.

If someone claims to have been a "security consultant" or "former intelligence officer," seek verification. You can use these folks, but know who they are and how they make their living. An amazing number of these experts trace their sources back to a handful of founding fathers of this cottage industry, folks with questionable credentials and spurious reputations. Be a skeptic. That's true also of the government's terrorism investigations. Muslims have as much of an interest as anybody in seeing real bad guys brought to justice. They also have an interest in seeing that a defendant's rights are preserved. What's delivered by prosecutors at a press conference after an arrest doesn't always show up before a jury at a trial. As journalists, doing our jobs well and with unflinching allegiance to the truth helps not only Muslims but also our communities and our country.

ASK A MUSLIM

Your best sources and keys to understanding Muslims are Muslims themselves. A good caution here is to remember that Muslims aren't monolithic. As with any faith, there are different interpretations and levels of orthodoxy. A great resource is the cache of polling data about Muslims that has been amassed by the Pew Forum on Religion & Public Life (pewforum.org).

But nothing replaces the confidence a reporter gets from having spent time with your subjects. Before I wrote a six-part series called "United By Faith" for the *St. Petersburg Times*, I spent nine months attending Friday prayers at a local mosque and did dozens of interviews. I visited Muslims in their homes, at their businesses, at Fourth of July picnics, on Muslim holidays, and at their kids' soccer games. I ate meals with local Muslims. I got to know multiple generations of Muslims: the first immigrants from countries like Syria and Egypt, the children they brought with them, and the children and grandchildren who were born here and who have grown up in American schools.

At the *Indianapolis Star*, I have written about one of the most prominent American Muslim institutions, the Islamic Society of North America, which is based just outside of Indianapolis. To get to know them better, I interviewed all their leaders and studied their history and what the cottage industry of "experts" have said about them. I also spent three-day weekends attending their national conventions on three successive years. I've attended their lectures, met their supporters from around the country, and even shopped at their convention's bazaar. From all that, I came to understand the organization, its history, and its sometimes awkward relationship with the federal government. I also came to see that much of what was written about them by the cottage industry of "experts" was largely divorced from reality. All of which brings us to my next tip.

Go Where Your Reporting Leads You

Let your reporting lead you where it will, even when the place you are headed is unpopular. Like that river current, reporters are pulled by the tug of conventional wisdom, by the slanders of the Islamophobes, or, worse yet, by our own laziness. We must be better than that.

At the *St. Petersburg Times*, I was introduced to the Muslim community while investigating the background of a man who had been arrested on terrorism charges. I staked out his house, knocked on the doors of anybody who knew him, and called around the country. In other words, I looked at the case against a suspect and I wrote about it.

But in doing that work I also found a whole new line of leads about a Muslim community that our newspaper had written virtually nothing about. The terrorism suspect was one person in a Muslim community of hundreds, including many who were quiet pillars in medical and other fields. The series I eventually wrote for the *St. Petersburg Times* told the story of immigrants who arrived in the 1970s, filled important gaps in the medical needs of the county, and eventually grew to dozens of families. It was rich with details about their lives and hopes and dreams.

In the same way, while attending the Islamic Society's convention in Columbus, Ohio, I picked up a tip that a Muslim congressional candidate from Indianapolis was holding a political fundraiser. I took off through the suburbs of Columbus in search of it. I found the fundraiser, found my Muslim congressional candidate, and found the people who were there to write him large checks. More importantly, I found an unexpected story, one that went against the current. It was a story of Muslims—both immigrants and American-born Muslims—who not only believe in the democratic process, but who had figured out how to play the game. I found the story because I followed the leads where they took me.

Build Sources

Building sources in the Muslim community can, at times, be trickier than on other beats. Muslims have been under the microscope for a decade now. They've seen some good reporting and plenty of breathless sensationalism. For a long time Muslims were being asked for their response to every terrorist atrocity committed abroad or here at home. You could just see the fatigue in their eyes from having to answer the same questions again and again. After a while, many grew weary of the media and some remain so. The remedy for this is to get to know your local Muslim communities outside of crisis. Yes, you can start with the obligatory Ramadan fasting and iftar stories. But use those as a doorway to make contacts and to pick up other story ideas. Come back weeks after Ramadan and follow up with a story about something else going on in the Muslim community, or write a profile of an interesting personality you meet. Still not getting anywhere? Look for younger members of the Muslim community. They are often the most willing to engage the media. They also may be carrying less cultural baggage than the immigrants who came before them. Some from the older generation may have lived most of their lives under repressive regimes that wouldn't tolerate free media. They may be more inclined to circle the wagons.

The second and third generations have been consumers of American media their whole lives. They get what you're doing. And many of them understand the value of good public relations and that building a fence doesn't help the cause of understanding. Once you find the people who can usher you in, you can help your new sources grow in confidence that you are a serious journalist who will do good work. How? By showing you are a good listener. Ask questions that show you're trying to understand and do responsible reporting. After being yelled at and having phones hung up in my ear early in my reporting on Muslims at the *St. Petersburg Times*, I was eventually greeted by Muslim leaders as "the Christian who loves Muslims." I had done nothing to compromise my journalistic principles. I had merely shown that I could be trusted. I came to hear Muslims telling other Muslims they could trust me. It was gratifying, but more importantly it made the journalism easier. It made it possible to find the stories that went several levels deeper.

Understand Muslim Diversity

The diversity of the Muslim community can be truly surprising, and it's important to understand its breadth. I've talked a lot so far about immigrant Muslims, who were the focus of my reporting at the *St. Petersburg Times*. But upon coming to the Midwest to be the religion writer for the *Indianapolis Star*, I found worlds of diversity. There are black Muslims, white American-born Muslim converts, and Hispanic Muslims. There are nonobservant

Muslims, gay Muslims, feminist Muslims, and the Nation of Islam, which most orthodox Muslims wouldn't consider Muslims at all. Even among immigrant groups, the countries of origin influence their practice of the faith. Muslims from the Middle East could have much different views on matters like clothing, gender relations, or even alcohol than Muslims from Indonesia or western Africa. There are other factors to consider too. Not all Arabs are Muslims. There's a decent number of Arab Christians in the United States, and many of them share the same concerns about American foreign policy and civil liberties issues.

Then there is the diversity among Muslim women. This is most readily apparent with fashion. Some wear scarves to cover their heads, veils to cover their faces, and loose-fitting clothing to obscure their figures. Most go several degrees less than that. Some wear just a headscarf or loose-fitting clothes. Other Muslim women go without a head covering at all and buy their clothes off the rack at Target or emulate the pages of *Vogue*. The key thing is not to assume that fashion choices equate to a certain amount of religious devotion. Many of these distinctions are based on regional customs. The reasons a woman gives for her choices of attire often say much about her. And while we're talking about gender issues, male reporters may sometimes find different degrees of access to the women in Muslim communities. Some women will speak to you at any place at any time, others only in the presence of others or in front of their husbands. Still others won't speak to a male nonrelative at all. In these cases, male reporters may need to bring in a female reporter to assist. Don't judge. Don't bemoan. Just do what's needed to tell a story. It may be that access issues become part of your story.

VITAL WORK

Reporting on American Muslims right now is vital work. Where religious extremism exists, there is an important security concern. But the larger story is about how this community is finding its place in American society. Some older black Muslims liken this period to the 1960s civil rights movement. Yes there is less violence and no lynchings, but there are still prejudices and obstacles. Muslims, like Catholics, Jews, and other faith groups before them, are still working on full acceptance. There's little doubt that how journalists "represent" Muslims will influence their progress.

Robert King is a journalist with the *Indianapolis Star*. He reported on lives of Muslims in America in the wake of 9/11 and continues to follow how Muslim Americans navigate politics, faith, and family.

TEN

MUSLIMS IN THE MEDIA: CHALLENGES AND REWARDS OF REPORTING ON MUSLIMS

Ammina Kothari

MENTION A MUSLIM WOMAN IN the Western media and audiences imagine a burka-clad or hijab-wearing woman. Read a story about terrorism and Western media audiences expect to see a bearded, angry-looking man. Why are Muslim women oppressed? What makes Muslim men violent? These are representative of some of the questions I get asked every time I teach a class about media coverage of Muslims, give a guest lecture, or present my research at national conferences on Islam-related issues. When I explain that not all or even many Muslim women are oppressed or Muslim men violent, someone invariably points to a story in the media as evidence to support their perception of Muslims.

As a Muslim woman who had been studying in the United States for a year before the 9/11 attacks, I am keenly aware of how perceptions of Muslims shifted in the eyes of Americans and forced me to adapt my own identity and constantly reflect on how I present myself and my religious/cultural upbringing. During the past ten years, I have searched for media examples that reflect my experiences but instead I have—too often—found stories related to violence and oppression. These media stories have created and are sustaining an environment that exacerbates cultural differences and promulgates stereotypical mindsets. It is increasingly important to train future producers of media messages to develop a nuanced cultural understanding and to be able to penetrate the veneer of common stereotypes.

Muslim men and women represent a wide variety of experiences in the United States. We are migrants and American-born. We work as educators, journalists, doctors, engineers, lawyers, and clerical workers, and we own businesses. Some of us are stricter followers of Islamic teachings compared to those more moderate in their beliefs and practices; still others of us are culturally influenced but nonpracticing. For many Americans, however, Muslims represent a monolithic group; these representations are often acquired via the media's focus on Islam as an identity maker, diluting the diversity of cultures and the spectrum of belief systems.

JOURNALIST SHAPE UNDERSTANDING (AND MISUNDERSTANDING)

Journalists, through their news source preferences and selection of certain information, play an important role in shaping what news audiences consume and how they understand and interpret issues and events related to Muslims. While the media's objective may be to report news without bias, objectives are often subject to the realities of the newsroom. Shrinking resources and a high-pressure environment in which "newsworthy" stories must be delivered on a tight deadline add extra challenges. Often stories produced in this environment employ religion as a news hook. Journalists who are not aware of Islam in larger contexts struggle to find sources that provide multiple perspectives. A story about Muslims or Islam that could have been written with more balanced nuances becomes more hackneyed as a result.

Another potential pitfall in portrayals of different cultures in the news, especially in the arena of politically oriented media, is the absence of cultural nuance in news stories. Media practitioners are trained to ask questions and seek answers but, in the rush to meet deadlines, can neglect sources and perspectives from varied cultural backgrounds.

I have close and persistent ties with family in Africa and Asia, so when I read the news, I constantly try to find a balance of perspectives in stories that focus on the global-US connections, especially in the political arena. Although in some instances it is not feasible for the media to incorporate global perspectives in the news, there is a palpable neglect of nuanced domestic sources, those connected in immediate and intimate ways with multiple cultures. This is evident even when considering news generated in student publications in a globalized college campus like Indiana University.

Creating Meaningful Classroom Experiences

During the four years I worked on my doctoral degree at Indiana University, I had the good fortune to have many opportunities to speak to a number of undergraduate classes and teach courses about Muslims in the media. I was invited to speak to classes as a guest lecturer and asked to provide perspective on the issues surrounding the representation of Muslims in the media. This informed and shaped my own understanding of Islam and Muslims as understood by others through the media lens. When an opportunity to design a research course on Muslims representations in the media presented itself, I realized a unique opportunity, as an educator, to help improve the existing coverage of Muslims in the US media by training future journalists.

In my course design, I divided the schedule into two sections: the first focused on an exploration of the diversity in the Muslim community with firsthand news reporting by the students, and the second concentrated on media analysis using interdisciplinary literature and drawing from students' reporting experiences. My goal was to introduce students to invaluable resources available on the university campus in the form of scholars and individuals, including Muslim students from around the US and the world, who would be able to provide varied perspective in and about news stories. The students were given freedom to select a topic and sources to interview, with the caveat that they must interview at least one Muslim source for their story. The goal of this assignment was to introduce students to one or more members of a group that most of them had seen marginalized, stereotyped, and even vilified in the media.

The news story assignment was a learning process both for the students and for me. It highlighted the challenges faced by journalists on a daily basis as they attempted to report on either Islam or Muslims, both of which are diverse. An added complication is the environment created by recent global events and sensationalized media coverage, which has made many Muslims reluctant to give interviews to the media, even if the interviewers are student journalists. When I asked students to reflect on the reporting experience, they shared a new appreciation for journalists who have to find willing sources under a tight deadline and make sure the story has news value to sell. The students admitted that when they were successful in securing an interview with a Muslim source, their understanding of the story they were pursuing was significantly changed, and in the few cases where the students were unable to convince their preferred Muslim sources to grant them an interview, they realized how the missing voices limited the story. Some of the stories written by my students focused on topics such as efforts to unite Jewish and Muslim communities on Indiana's campus, a contemporary take on hijab, experiences of Iraqi refugees in Syria, and women's rights in Saudi Arabia. While the students wrote the stories for the class, their willingness to have them published and disseminated to a wider audience fulfilled a larger journalistic goal: some of the stories published on the *Muslim Voices* blog led to an informed dialogue among readers, who appreciated coverage of stories usually ignored by mainstream media, and the inclusion of Muslim voices.

Together with excellent reporting and writing proficiency, journalism students need critical thinking skills to have a successful media career. The media analysis portion of the course focused on honing their research skills in many areas, including how to search for appropriate academic sources to support an argument, how to select an appropriate method for media analysis, and how to write a coherent analytical research paper. During the course of the two semesters when I taught the courses "Muslims and the Media" and "Muslims in the Media" at Indiana University, I found that students researched and gained extensive knowledge about a particular issue—related to a specific Muslim community, country, or culture—when they were personally curious to learn more about the subject. The freedom to collaboratively explore and collectively critique what we considered mistakes allowed our class to learn new concepts in a participatory manner. Four of the research papers written by my students were selected for presentation at the Re-scripting Islam: Muslims and the Media conference, which took place on March 23 and 24, 2011, at Indiana University. The papers' focus ranged from analysis of the media's portrayal of Jordan in Israeli-Palestinian peacemaking, Muslims in sports, Islam in hip-hop, and female journalists in Saudi Arabia.

A SAFE SPACE FOR CONVERSATION

The experience of teaching courses related to Muslim representations in the media made me think about how my own background and identity significantly affects both the content of the course and class discussions. I became especially aware that my own identity affects students' responses in collaborative work when they have to express opinions or ask questions out loud. Initially I found that students were reluctant to ask questions they perceived to be personal or critical of Islam, which required me to come up with strategies that would encourage them to use the classroom as a learning resource and a safe place to ask questions. I had students write down questions anonymously at the beginning of the class based on the reading for the day, and during the class I addressed their questions. Creating an open-discussion environment required me to open myself up to criticism and questions of a more personal nature about my beliefs and religious practices. For instance, when we discussed the topic of hijab and burka, students wanted to know my perspective on the issue. As someone who wears a form of hijab or *ridha* when attending a religious gathering at a mosque, my answer was confusing to some, who only saw me as an instructor in Western clothes. I had to clarify that such clothes and religious coverings are culturally defined and that the reasons for wearing them vary as well. Some men and women wear Islamic clothes to express their religious identity, for others the religious clothes signify their cultural and national identity, which are often a blend of religion and culture. For many others, wearing clothes with religious connotation is a sign for respect for the occasion, such as attending prayers at a mosque or events at an Islamic center. While it was challenging sometimes to be a spokesperson for a diverse religion such as Islam and have class discussions that forced me to simultaneously play the role of moderator and the subject of the learning, at the end of the semester I was rewarded by students' evaluations, many of which noted appreciation for the opportunity to ask questions in a safe environment and a teacher who was willing to be challenged and interrogated about her faith and cultural beliefs.

Looking at my handouts and lecture notes from those four years, I see how my own teaching style and knowledge about my religion has expanded. Due to these teaching opportunities, I had the opportunity to invite some nationally and globally respected journalists and scholars to speak to my class and for us to learn from them. My students' thoughtful questions in the class and for the guest speakers made me realize that social barriers and misunderstandings are a two-way street that require collaborative efforts to bridge. Americans who grew up in the post-9/11 world have a one-dimensional view of Muslims that is reinforced frequently in the media, which limits their ability to interact and empathize with issues faced by the followers of Islam. Muslims also have learned to hold their distance from people they perceive to be hostile toward their religion and culture. In order to build cultural understanding, each one of us has to take steps to bridge the divide. When I offered to teach the course on "Muslims in the Media," I opened myself to questions, and students who signed up for my classes were willing to confront their existing biases and to learn more about Muslims. This reaffirmed a central belief in humanity that I wanted to share: misunderstanding and divides can be bridged when there are individuals willing to take risks and take the first step.

It would be naïve to assume that a few courses focusing on analyses of media representations of Muslims in the Western media will change the dominant anti-Islamic bias in the United States, when there are plenty of media-savvy spokespersons willing to reinforce images of a monolithic, violent religion. But progress can be made in the presence of Americans willing and curious to learn about Muslims and in the presence of Muslims willing to share their experiences. I invite journalists, as I did my students, to reach out to Muslim communities often present in our own neighborhoods or check out the faculty, staff, and students on a campus close by. With the willingness to be open and persistent, we may find that almost everyone has a story to tell, which may provide not just new story ideas and leads but also local context for global issues often episodically covered in the media.

Ammina Kothari is an assistant professor in the School of Communication at Rochester Institute of Technology. She studies global communication and journalism practices, with a special focus on conflicts, health, gender, technology, and religion.

ELEVEN

NEW MEDIA AND MUSLIM VOICES

Rosemary Pennington

IT SHOULD HAVE BEEN AN afternoon like any other in Chapel Hill, North Carolina, home to one of the United States' most revered public universities. February 10, 2015, should have been mundane. Instead, with its close came the revelation that the lives of three young people characterized by their friends and family as compassionate and loving were taken by a neighbor.

Twenty-three-year-old Deah Barakat, twenty-one-year-old Yusor Mohammad Abu-Salha, and nineteen-year-old Razan Mohammad Abu-Salah were involved in various charities in their community. Deah Barakat had helped launch a fundraiser to cover the cost of dental care for Syrian refugee children. Deah was also a dental student at the University of North Carolina, where he'd be joined by his wife, Yusor, in the fall. Razan was a student at North Carolina State University. They were bright stars in their communities, with lives full of promise, until those lives were taken away by forty-six-year-old Craig Stephen Higgs. Higgs, with whom the three reportedly had had multiple negative interactions, walked into their home, shot each of them in the head, and then fled the scene. He later turned himself in to authorities, claiming the shooting was over a parking dispute, while Muslim communities, both in Chapel Hill and outside it, urged authorities to consider the mass murder a hate crime. The three bright young individuals killed that day in Chapel Hill were Muslim American.

After their murder, social media quickly filled with photographs of Deah, Yusor, and Razan. A few photos came from the day, just six weeks before their murder, Deah and Yusor married. A short video began circulating that showed Yusor, her face to the camera, sinking a three-point shot after throwing it behind her without looking. Another photo showed Razan in a cap and gown at graduation, Yusor and Deah standing next to her. Still another photo showed Yusor and Deah in the crowd of a University of North Carolina football game. The images and the stories from friends that were posted to Facebook, shared on Twitter, and reblogged in Tumblr framed the three as living the most American of lives.

While their Muslim identity was made visible in photos circulating after their deaths, also visible was how clearly all three had integrated into American culture. A number of the Muslim Tumblr users I have worked with in my research are a lot like the Chapel Hill three. Like Deah, Yusor, and Razan, the bloggers were born in the West. Like them, they are college students or hope to go to college. Like them, they are sports fans or write about fashion, as Razan did. They want their religious identities and their national identities to coexist; they do not want to be forced to have one take priority over the other. They want, as one Muslim Tumblr blogger wrote, to feel safe: "American Muslims represent the best of American society. How many of you know a Muslim doctor? A Muslim professor? A Muslim social worker? You know how many Muslims I meet who have Doctorates or are working on one? How many of you know of Muslims fundraising? We come from every single inch of this earth, showcasing hundreds of ethnicities and cultures that come together regardless. Muslims are nothing but amazing in America, yet Islamophobia is a real issue."

While much of the recent reporting on Muslims and new media has focused on the potential for radicalization, it has overlooked the ways Muslims use new media spaces to interrogate their faith, to create communities, and to connect to work toward social change. This chapter explores Islam online and considers how journalists can leverage new and social media to improve and contextualize their reporting on Muslim communities.

DETERRITORIALIZING CONNECTIONS

Media narratives help us navigate our world, help us decide who is dangerous and who is not. Media representation of individuals, groups, and places fuels our understanding of the imagined communities to which we feel we belong.[1] This has been a role media have long served, with Benedict Anderson noting that newspapers played an integral role in the shaping of early understandings of nationhood.[2] Journalists, then, had a hand early on in helping define who belonged within particular communities and who belonged outside them. There is a journalistic responsibility to ensure that the communities that appear in our reporting actually reflect the physical realities of where we work and live. Representation, fair and accurate representation, should be a goal journalists strive for in their work. Of course, as journalistic output moves from the printed page to broadcast airwaves to the digital realm, becoming more expansive along the way, and as ideas of community begin to expand beyond the physical, covering community accurately becomes more difficult. It becomes the work of reporters to not only understand the physical communities their interviewees and sources feel they belong to but to also consider what other digital or global communities with which they identify.

Members of religious communities have long felt a push-and-pull between their local, physical communities and the larger body of often global believers to which they feel they belong. Linda Woodhead suggests that territorial affiliations are becoming less important to religious individuals as they discover the ways new media technologies allow them to interact with a more expansive, global community.[3] Believers now have access to a multitude of perspectives on their faith. No longer are religious individuals trapped in situations in which only the most physically accessible interpretation of their faith is available to them; people can now look much further afield for interpretations and practices they find meaningful.[4]

Nabil Echchaibi, who contributed a chapter to this book, has explored the ways new media technologies allow Muslims to circumvent local religious authorities and find interpretations of Islam that feel true to them.[5] Saminaz Zaman suggests that the "democratization" of Islam made possible by the Internet "simultaneously transcends hyphenated territorial labels to include all Muslims and splinters this very group into a thousand communities based on interpretation."[6] Daniel Varisco points out that this leads to a multitude of understandings of Islam so that—just as with Muslim communities offline—it becomes impossible to say there is one Muslim experience online or even a singular interpretation of Islam.[7]

This is important as you begin to consider the Muslim communities you are covering. Do the individuals you interview consider themselves part of a physical community of believers, or do they feel connected to a more globally constructed community? Even exploring the idea of a globally constructed community can be problematic because, as Arsalan Iftikhar pointed out early in this volume, there is no monolithic Muslim experience or identity; if your interviewees say they belong to a global Muslim community, it's your job to ask which one. Who gets to be part of that community and who must sit outside it? How do new media technologies aid in the construction and maintenance of those boundaries? Which new media spaces are your sources using and why?

SOCIAL MEDIA

To talk of the Internet in the singular is to make the mistake of seeing it as one media space when, in fact, the Internet is more of an ecological media environment in which exist a number of different types of spaces. There are corporate websites and discussion spaces for everything from Tudor history to the latest NPR podcast. There are e-mail providers and blogging platforms such as WordPress or LiveJournal. With the advent of what's called the "social web" have come possibilities for interaction that lead to the development of social networking sites (SNSs).

danah boyd and Nancy Ellison define social networking sites as "web-based services that allow individuals to (1) construct a public or semi-public profile within a bounded system, (2) articulate a list of other users with whom they share a connection, and (3) view and traverse their list of connections and those made by others within the system."[8] Social networking sites allow users to create identities and then to connect to others, people they often already know, in the spaces. Websites like Tumblr, Facebook, and Twitter and apps such as Instagram and Snapchat can be considered social networking sites. Inherent in social networking sites is the idea of interactivity; people use the spaces to exchange ideas, jokes, memes, stories, and other aspects of their lives with people. Social networking sites can help create public spheres for debate and discussion where individuals can begin to challenge representations they feel are unfair, inaccurate, or prejudicial.

In my own research on the use of social media by Muslims, I found individuals who were seeking to create an understanding of Islam that felt true to their personal experience of the faith. Tumblr, in particular, was used as a space to interrogate religious teachings and interpretations as well as to work out what it means, for those bloggers, to be Muslim. Many of the Tumblr bloggers I worked with admitted that while those conversations were really meant for their own personal growth or for other Muslims in their networks, they were aware that non-Muslims might come across their posts. Helping non-Muslims get a better idea of the diversity of Islam became an important motivator for many of the bloggers' use of the space.

Tumblr and Twitter have also served as spaces in which to criticize and challenge the framing of Muslims in the news media. Muslim users of Twitter and Tumblr were often consciously using their personal accounts to engage in a broader public conversation about their faith. For many of them, it often felt like a hopeless undertaking given the history of misrepresentation of Muslims (as Peter Gottschalk and Rafia Zakaria have discussed in this book), but one they felt compelled to take part in to try to change the narrative of Muslims as dangerous, threatening outsiders. Simultaneously, the actions of the Islamic State are propelling a new wave of reporting focused on the possibility of a "Muslim threat."

THREAT OF RADICALIZATION

As mentioned earlier in this chapter, there has been an increased focus on Muslim use of social media as politicians and academics struggle to understand what leads to the radicalization of some individuals. This has become especially salient in light of the Islamic State's use of new media technologies to spread its message as well as recruit new members.

The important thing to remember is that media alone cannot do anything. Research has shown that media do not have a direct effect on people; just because a message exists and circulates does not mean it will radicalize someone. You have to consider how the message is framed, what type of media is used to communicate it, and to whom it is directed. If the message deals with something individuals haven't encountered before, it's not likely to be effective. If it is not relevant to an individual's life, then it's not likely to be effective. In relation to Internet media, Andrew Hoskins and Ben O'Loughlin have noted that "it is not clear that radicalization can be identified through analysis of online activity."[9] Explorations of the issue of radicalization must get beyond media use and media messages to be of any value to your audience. To focus on media alone in your reporting is to perpetuate a simplistic understanding of the concept.

You also have to be willing to interrogate the very idea of radicalization. What does it mean to be a radical? How is the process of an individual's radicalization framed? Peter Neumann points out that while scholars and others who study radicalization all agree it's a process—something that happens over time—there is still debate over what exactly constitutes radicalization, with people often split over how, or whether, to differentiate radical thoughts from radical behavior.[10] To cover the subject of radicalization well, you have to understand how the concept is being defined as well as who is being framed as radical.

Radicalization is a complicated process influenced by a number of things, including personal experiences, political contexts, socioeconomic status, experiences with social exclusion, and sometimes media, among other things.[11] As you report on individuals who have been radicalized, there are a number of questions you will want to consider. What was the individual's home life like? What was the individual's experience like at school? Is the society and culture where the individual grew up one of inclusion or exclusion? How has the individual experienced prejudice in his or her life? How religious is the individual? Is any religiosity the person may express new found or long held?

Only after you've begun to explore the broader context of an individual's life and experience should you begin to explore the way media have played into that person's possible radicalization. Media messages are only effective when they resonate with an individual on a personal level. Your job as a reporter is to figure out what it is about the message that made it resonate. What aspect of the message did the individual find so motivating that he or she decided to adopt a radical behavior? If you leave that context out of your reporting, you are doing your audience a major disservice and you are likely oversimplifying the story in a way that only solidifies stereotypes. As Shadi Hamid notes, "It's banal to say so, but different people are radicalized in different ways."[12] Your reporting should reflect that reality as much as possible.

Tools for Reporting

The reality of this "democratization" of Islam online and this diversity of Muslim experience in Internet spaces should make you realize there is no excuse for not having a diverse array of Muslim voices appear in your reporting. There are several new media strategies you can adopt when working the Islam beat in order to enrich your reporting. The first might be the simplest.

Create a List in Twitter

A Twitter list allows you to create a list of other accounts you find interesting and useful. Then, when you open up Twitter, you can click on the list and see what those specific people are saying. It organizes them away from your general timeline, making it easy to follow particular groups of people or topics.

If you are covering Muslim communities or writing stories about Islam, you should create a Twitter list. There are a wide variety of Muslims who are using Twitter, everyone from imams to academics to just everyday believers, and finding those who are in your coverage area and following them will give you an idea of what's happening in the community or what the community is concerned about. One of the criticisms pundits like to trot out whenever a terrorist attack happens is the line, "Where are the Muslims condemning these actions?" A Twitter list will give you instant access to Muslim reaction.

If you actually interact with the people on the list, it could also be a useful way of cultivating sources in the community. Reporters are only as good as the sources they cultivate; if you are covering Muslim communities, a Twitter list is one way of working on that cultivation.

Pay Attention to Hashtags (Across Social Media)

As you may be well aware, people in social media often rally around particular hashtags to draw attention to an issue or controversy. The #blacklivesmatter hashtag is a good example of an activist movement growing up around a hashtag. Not every hashtag will have the power to produce a movement, but they are a way to create a public conversation around a topic, with many of them used by activists and individuals across social media platforms.

Often, news outlets will follow hashtags that arise in relation to an event and publish social media posts using the hashtag in news stories on their websites or in stories in their broadcasts. While that is one way to use hashtags in reporting, another way is to use the hashtags to find people who might be sources for stories about the topic of the hashtag or for other stories in the future. Following hashtags is also a good way to get an idea of what sort of consensus might be developing around an issue or to gauge how the conversation is changing. Don't just look at hashtags for material to be farmed for stories. Also think about how they can introduce you to potential sources that will help diversify and contextualize your reporting in the future.

Like Facebook Pages (or Similar Pages in Similar Sites)

A number of organizations have pages in spaces like Facebook to communicate with their audiences and community members. (*Muslim Voices*, the media arm of The Voices and Visions Project that facilitated this volume is one such organization.) If you "Like" the page, then you get updates about the organization's activities as well as get an idea of what issues are of concern to them.

When thinking about how to leverage social media in your reporting, consider finding the Facebook pages of local mosques or Muslim groups in your coverage area. You will see what events are coming up, what holidays are important, when any open houses are scheduled at mosques, as well as see what outreach the organization is engaged in, which could give you story ideas. You'll also often be able to see who else has liked the organization, which could help you widen your list of sources you can turn to when working on a story related to Islam or a Muslim community.

Be Ethical in Your Use of Social Media

Do not pull tweets, Facebook posts, Tumblr posts, Instagram posts, or any other type of social media content without first asking the creator's permission. Social media can feel as though it is a public space and, as journalists, we are taught that things in public view are generally ours to report on. People who use social media, however, often do so with some expectation of privacy and with a sense of ownership of their posts. It can feel like an invasion of privacy when people see their tweets or Facebook posts appear in news stories without their permission. So, be sure send the person whose post you'd like to use a private or direct message asking for permission. This will have the added benefit of possibly giving you a source to go back to with questions or help with stories in the future.

This is actually a step you should adopt whenever you are considering using social media content in your reporting, but it is especially important when covering marginalized communities, whether that marginalization arises from religion, ethnicity, gender, or some other aspect of identity. When you are repeatedly the subject of stereotype and prejudice, it can be disempowering to see your words, ideas, or thoughts taken without your permission to fill a hole in a news story. The Society of Professional Journalists' (SPJ) Code of Ethics[13] tells journalists to "Boldly tell the story of diversity and magnitude of the human experience. Seek sources whose voices we seldom hear" as well as to "minimize harm" in their reporting. Taking someone's social media material without their permission and making it accessible to a broader public than the user envisioned when creating or sharing that material is in direct opposition to the quoted SPJ principles. If we are to cover communities responsibly, if we are to gain the trust of sources and our audiences, we must not only avoid perpetuating stereotypes in our reporting, but we also must respect the people we hope to quote in our work.

Journalism is a practice that relies on human interaction to be successful. Don't look at social media as a way to avoid those interactions but instead as a way to make them more fruitful. Michael Schudson famously wrote, "Journalism never stands entirely outside the community it reports on."[14] When covering Muslim communities, social media can help you better reflect that community. In the case of the Chapel Hill shootings, reporters were able to use social media to bring to life the stories of three young adults and help their audience begin to understand what life is like for some Muslim Americans. The photos and videos journalists used in their reporting showed Deah, Yusor, and Razan living the most American of lives; though both Yusor and Razan wore hijab, what was most noticeable in the images was not their dress, but instead their smiles and the joy with which they seemed to approach life. When used thoughtfully and ethically by journalists, social media can help us see into the lives of others.

Rosemary Pennington is Assistant Professor of Journalism at Miami University. Since 2008 she has been involved with Indiana University's Voices and Visions project, serving as project coordinator, podcast producer, and managing editor.

MUSLIM VOICES

ONE

FAIZ RAHMAN:
UNDERSTANDING WILL TAKE TIME

http://purl.dlib.indiana.edu/iudl/media/j23603rw8d

In 2008, Faiz Rahman, then president of the Bloomington Islamic Center, told the story of how his neighbors responded to his family after the September 11th terrorist attacks.

❁

As an immigrant family, we tried to put ourselves in other people's shoes. We knew we were different and that some people might feel uneasy with our color, accent, or my wife's long dresses and her Islamic headscarf.

So, I called my wife and asked how everything was. If our two boys, at that time aged four and two, were okay. If anyone called or knocked on the door. She said the kids were okay and there were knocks on the door and also phone calls.

I felt a cold snap passing through my spine.

"Who are they?"

She calmly said, "Our neighbors."

"Which ones? Did they say anything? Or leave anything? Did they leave any message?" I almost screamed.

"Yes," she said. "One knocked on the door. I was scared and didn't respond, but then that neighbor called from her home and left a message saying they're worried about us. She said we can stay with them tonight if we feel scared or vulnerable. Two others also left messages, they said similar things . . ." My wife couldn't finish her sentence, her voice almost choked with emotion.

Well, I was amazed. I wasn't ready for this. I thought the knocks and calls came from people who wanted to kick us out, not to invite us to stay with them if we are scared.

Change Happens Slowly

Well, seven years have passed since that fateful morning of 9/11. Many things have changed in our country since then, some for the better, some for the worse, but for Muslims in America it continues to be a rollercoaster ride.

Within a few days of the terrorist attack, thousands of Muslims had been rounded up by the federal authorities in an effort to identify potential terrorists. Many have been in prison for months or years, others deported, but none has been convicted of any crime.

At the same time, many sympathetic Americans across the country have taken the extra step of visiting mosques, participating in interfaith dialogues, and making new Muslim friends. But, unfortunately, ignorance still persists and the number of hate crimes against Muslims has gone up in recent years.

On the upside, though, Muslims in recent years have been elated at the election of the first ever Muslim to the US Congress and even more elated at the election of the second one. These events have somehow assured them that they still have a place in their own country and that the good old American virtues of fairness and justice will finally triumph over the ugly human vices of stereotype and prejudice. Although the false rumors in recent months about the Democratic presidential nominee being a secret Muslim and that this is considered a negative by some raises doubts, again, in the minds of many American Muslims.

Can a Muslim truly be considered an American like any other?

Well, if my neighbor's actions on 9/11 are any indication, then the answer has to be yes. It's just going to take honest dialogue, a lot of understanding, and time.

TWO

SOHAIB SULTAN:
WHAT MUSLIMS BELIEVE

http://purl.dlib.indiana.edu/iudl/media/p88c484t52

It's not difficult to find misunderstandings about Islam. A Google search un-
covers page after page of misinformation about the faith. Like any religion,
there are facets to Islam; people may practice in different ways but the core
beliefs of Islam are the same no matter where or who you are.

Sohaib Sultan has worked on university campuses and done public outreach for years. No question asked about Islam surprises him anymore.

"My general experience is that people ask questions truly wanting to
know and they don't ask it out of wanting to offend or anything like that,"
Sultan said. "By now I've received so many questions that no question really
catches me off guard."

THE BASICS OF ISLAM

Sultan is a Muslim chaplain at Princeton University as well as the author of
two books, *The Koran for Dummies* and *The Qur'an and Sayings of Prophet
Muhammad*. Sultan says there are six core beliefs in Islam, but the one that
defines the faith is the belief in the oneness of God.

"That's at the foundation of Islam. When it comes to Islamic spirituality
the oneness of God is essential. When it comes to ethics, the oneness of God
is essential. I would take that as being the entire message of the Qur'an and

the entire message of Islam," explains Sultan. "That there is no god but God, there is no deity worthy of worship but the one God."

He says there seems to be a lot of confusion over Allah in the minds of some outside Islam. Sultan says there are even those who think Allah is a pagan moon god, which is not the case. He says that Allah is simply the one God and was never anything else.

Peace, Not War

Confusion over Allah is far from the only misperception over the faith. Probably the most widely held, Sultan says, is the idea that jihad equals holy war.

"We know that there's a big misperception around the term jihad," Sultan said. "This idea that jihad is this wanton violence, that it's vigilante kidnapping and bombing and so on and so forth. Whereas jihad just means struggle. It means to struggle in the path of God. And this takes many, many different forms. Anything from building a soup kitchen to raising a family. This is all part of a struggle to obtain the good pleasure of God."

That's not to say that jihad can't entail armed conflict. But, Sultan says, it's a defensive measure, not an offensive one. A jihad that only a state or a government can perform. And, he adds, jihad should never be used as a defense of terrorism. Sultan says that kind of vigilantism is not condoned anywhere in Islam.

Which leads to the one thing he hopes people will understand about Islam if they understand nothing else: that the faith is one based on peace.

"Islam is about creating the internal peace with God. It's about creating a social system that allows people to live in safety and security and peace. This is what the vision of Islam is all about. This is what the ideal of Islam is all about," Sultan said.

Sultan says that message can get lost, but, he says, he feels certain if people dig deep, if they look past the stereotypes of Muslims and Islam, they'll see the faith for what it really is.

THREE

HEATHER AKOU:
THE VEIL

http://purl.dlib.indiana.edu/iudl/media/x913667d2z

It is among the most recognizable aspects of Islam, the veil, but what is it exactly and what does it entail? The Qur'an states simply that women and men are to dress modestly. Some have interpreted this as meaning women must cover their heads with a scarf outside the home. For others, it has meant that women must cover themselves from head to toe in garments like the blue burka of Afghanistan. Heather Akou is an associate professor at Indiana University and expert in African and Muslim dress. She's also a Muslim who wears a headscarf. Rosemary Pennington spoke with Akou in 2008 about the veil.

Heather Akou: So, usually, when people talk about the veil today they're talking specifically about Muslim head coverings and, I guess, for me personally and for a lot of Muslims the term "veil" is actually not very helpful. Really, what people prefer to call it is hijab, which actually means covering and it refers to a whole set of practices involving modesty of the body and not necessarily a specific item of dress.

Rosemary Pennington: So when you talk about hijab, what exactly is that? Is that a specific idea of what hijab is or is it a cultural thing?

HK: Well, the idea of hijab is actually very general. The word "hijab" itself means covering, and it refers not only to covering the body but also, for example, if you think about a screen within your house that could also be referred to as hijab because you're using it to hide, perhaps, people behind the screen or screen off one part of the room. So it is actually a very, very general word. Now, if you think about "how did it get applied to certain items of clothing," specifically covering the head, the Qur'an says, basically, people should dress modestly, cover your private parts. And that's really about all it says. Now, it does specifically use the word hijab but it doesn't say you have to wear black, it doesn't say you should cover your face, in fact it doesn't really say what parts of your body you should cover, just that you should cover your "private parts." So that really leaves the door open to a lot of interpretation. So, for instance, in Afghanistan where you saw women wearing head to toe body coverings, you can't even see their face, their face is actually hidden behind a screen so they can see out and you can't see in. That is very much a cultural interpretation. In fact, there are lot of Muslims that think that's pretty extreme and it's pretty degrading to women. So, it's definitely not a universal thing that all Muslims think is good practice.

RP: What do you say to those people who think hijab and having women wearing headscarves is an oppressive thing?

HK: To a certain extent I can understand how people have come to the idea that wearing a headscarf is oppressive, especially when you think about a case like Afghanistan; definitely women were being oppressed and are still being oppressed. I mean, not being allowed to hold a job outside your home or go to school, to have young children growing up with no education because you have some very extreme ideas about sheltering them; that is oppressive. So I'm not surprised Americans and people in other parts of the West have really gotten this idea that covering your head is oppressive, but I wish more Americans knew that covering the body and being modest actually has a much longer history in common not just to Islam but also to Judaism and Christianity, and in many other religions around the world there's a very common idea of covering your private parts, being modest about your body. That's really where the practice started. The idea was not to oppress women; in fact, many Muslim women see it as being very liberating. That other people are not looking at them thinking, "Oh, what do I think about her haircut or her makeup." You're covering your body and of course you can display it when you're at home, it's not that you have no body and you have no beauty, but outside the home you don't want to be an object of harassment. You want to have people interact with you based on your ideas and your abilities and not so much what you look like.

FOUR

SHEIDA RIAHI:
ARABIC AND PERSIAN CALLIGRAPHY

http://purl.dlib.indiana.edu/iudl/media/d66v936483

Calligraphy is considered by many the highest form of Islamic art. Many calligraphers strive to beautify written Arabic to make it worthy of god, but it's not only Arabic that has entranced calligraphers; Persian is another language artists have attempted to beautify. Sheida Riahi is from Isfahan, an ancient city in Iran. Riahi studied calligraphy with a master in Iran before studying Islamic art at Indiana University. She explained to Rosemary Pennington why calligraphy has become so important to her.

Sheida Riahi: It was almost eight years ago that I went to the community of calligraphers in Iran, and they have a big school of calligraphy and I had a master there. I started practicing Nas'taliq, one of the Persian styles of calligraphy, and then I switched to Tuluth, which is one of the Arabic styles of calligraphy, and I really liked it because with that calligraphy I could write Qur'anic verses and it helped me to memorize those verses and it's very beautiful.

Rosemary Pennington: When you are practicing calligraphy, I've heard people say that in a way, for them, it's one of many ways to become closer to Allah and to understand the religion better. Is that what it's like to you? When you are practicing calligraphy is it not only an art form but a religious thing as well?

SR: To answer your question, I can say yes and no; it depends on what you're writing. If you are writing Persian poetry it's not directly related to religion, but what I can say is when you are practicing an art, especially a sacred art like calligraphy in Islam or maybe in Chinese tradition, you go to another world. You somehow disconnect yourself from all the crowds of this world and then you have a peace in your mind and if you are really aware of what's happening to you, you can concentrate on Allah. If you write the name of Allah, he is present in his name. So you have the direct connection with that name. But if you are not aware and you are just doing it as fun, some people would say . . . of course, it helps you, it makes you calmer, but it doesn't have anything to do with religion. It really depends on your perspective and your attitude toward the practice of calligraphy.

RP: Do you have any of your calligraphy that we could look at this morning?

SR: Certainly, yes, I can show you. This one is my calligraphy. I've written it in an Arabic style to write Persian calligraphy to see what it looks like because when you write Persian in Arabic style you don't have all the vowels, so it doesn't look as glorious as this piece of Arabic because it has all the vowels, and, in this case, it's all in red and it's very elaborate and so it looks very beautiful. I wrote this piece of Persian poetry in Arabic and it doesn't look that gorgeous. Unfortunately, I cannot say that I am an artist, but everything that I make I make it for gifts, so I give it away.

RP: You don't think that you're an artist?

SR: Well, I have practiced it and I really like it, but, well, I'm not a master.

RP: So when you're writing your calligraphy, it seems like you have to be very connected to language to be able to do this well. But, then, it seems like it is also very much a pursuit of beauty.

SR: Certainly, yes. I completely agree with you. That's true. Just knowing the language doesn't help if you don't know what you're writing. For me, I have practiced a little bit of Chinese characters. It's beautiful, it's very refreshing, but I don't understand anything, but I'm sure a master of Chinese calligraphy would enjoy it much better.

FIVE

ZAINEB ISTRABADI:
THE SUFI

http://purl.dlib.indiana.edu/iudl/media/247d76t17d

All three Abrahamic faiths have a mystical side to them. For Jews, there is Kabbalah; for Christians, the Gnostics; for Muslims, there are the Sufi. While the Sufi believe they are on a path toward becoming close to God after death, they also believe they can become close to God in this life, devoting energy to doing things for the love of God. But just as Islam itself is diverse, so is Sufism, with different orders pursuing different paths to divine unity, says Indiana University's Zaineb Istrabadi.

Zaineb Istrabadi: They engage in activities to cleanse the heart so that God, who cannot fit into anything, can fit into the heart of his believing servant, that's what Islamic tradition says. But you do not invite a king into a dirty stable, you invite him into a shining, clean palace. So the Sufis engage in activities to cleanse their heart, and there are techniques, including the remembrance of God.

Rosemary Pennington: When you say they are doing these things to cleanse themselves, what are they doing?

ZI: They engage, for example, in following the virtues in a very conscious way. They also engage in the repetition of some of the divine names, if not the name of God in Arabic, Allah, so there will be this repetition of "Allah, Allah, Allah" which you will hear, or the formula repeated, "There is no divinity except God." So this is like putting brasso on a brass vase that has been tarnished and you're wiping until the surface; at first it might get blackened even more and then as you keep wiping away and you keep buffing, then suddenly it starts shining and it reflects light. So it is with these mantras if you will, it brings the heart to life. Now I don't know if you've noticed, but when the Jews engage in prayer, if you see them at the synagogue or standing at the Wailing Wall, their bodies will sort of naturally move while they are doing their prayers. So it is with these mantras. They are very, very rhythmic. So in some orders, they're not really sects, they're orders, they have different sort of rules or techniques in the same way that the Franciscan and the Dominican and so on orders are generally the same, but they have specific rules.

RP: I've been doing some reading about Sufism, and I've been coming across the debate over whether Sufis are actually Muslims, where it seems like there are some who believe that instead of being a part of Islam that they're actually an offshoot of Islam. How did that view of Sufism come about?

ZI: Sufism, in my opinion, is absolutely part of Islamic tradition. In my opinion, anybody who says, "There is no divinity except God and Muhammad is his messenger," with all of the implications of those two statements, that that person is a Muslim. I, personally, am not interested in the details of how they practice; it is the Almighty who is going to be the ultimate judge. Having said that, there's no doubt that there are some things that Sufis do that appear to be outside of Islamic tradition, but I would not throw away or throw out the baby with the bathwater. There are some valid criticisms to be made, but I think those Muslims who say that Sufis are not Muslims are treading on dangerous ground. That is a very dangerous accusation to make in my opinion, and it is better to err on the side of "everyone is my brother" rather than to pick and choose.

SIX

UZMA MIRZA:
THE ROLE OF WOMEN IN ISLAM

http://purl.dlib.indiana.edu/iudl/media/v33r86c844

The role of women in Islam is a heated topic. On Internet message boards, in college classrooms, and even on the street the mere mention of those two words, "women" and "Islam," produces a strong reaction, both from those who see Islam as a force for equality and from those who see the religion as oppressive to women.

Fort Wayne, Indiana–based Uzma Mirza considers herself a thoroughly Westernized Muslim woman. In her roles as artist, architect, and philanthropist, Mirza says she's constantly trying to find her place in the world and to reconcile her faith in Islam with her sense of self. This is her reflection on her experience as a Muslim woman.

❧

All my work, my art, my architecture, my writing, it's all woven to actually critique yourself and that's the hardest thing. I was always adamant since I was five that there has to be a god because that is the only thing that safeguards who I am, not just as a Muslim woman, but a human being. The pool of water is constantly being stirred; there's no stagnancy, and generally, religion has this tendency to be stagnant except for Islam, in its integral aspect and the sayings of the Prophet Muhammad (peace be upon him),

whom Muslims consider the final brick in the wall of prophets. Adam, Abraham, Noah, and Jesus to Prophet Muhammad, they all spoke about wom-
en's rights, safeguarding the ill, the sick, the woman, the orphan, orphan's
property.

PROPHET'S EXAMPLE

Now, the Prophet was against anybody abusing women's rights. A chapter
in the Qur'an speaks about women. A woman gets up and basically tells the
Prophet about how her husband is treating her. I believe today's Muslim
men are hijacking Islam, many of them; not even just Muslim, even non-
Muslims, and this problem is not a religious problem, this problem is actually a human problem. You have to separate between Islam and the Prophet's teaching and what Muslims do. And today I think the Muslim men are
squeezing women so much that I've been told to leave mosque from a floor
by a certain man, but another man defended me by quoting a sunnah of the
Prophet, and he kept quiet and I kept praying. I didn't listen to him.

I stand for women's issues in the likeness of all prophets. You name one
prophet who did not do that? Actually, the prophets are the only people in
history who stood up for women's and men's and the orphan's and the el-
derly rights. Who else has done so much for standing up for human rights?

We blame God, we blame religion. Why don't we blame ourselves?

SEVEN

ANDRE CARSON:
LIFE AS A MUSLIM POLITICIAN

http://purl.dlib.indiana.edu/iudl/media/p29029q835

Out of the 535 lawmakers in the US Congress, only two are Muslim, both serving in the House of Representatives. The first, Keith Ellison, was elected from Minnesota in 2006. The second, from Indiana, is André Carson. He followed Ellison into the house two years later.

Carson was elected in a special election to fill the Seventh US District seat vacated by the death of his grandmother, Julia Carson. Julia Carson had held the seat for ten years before passing away. The congressman told Rosemary Pennington in 2009 that following his grandmother into the family business was a kind of calling.

Andre Carson: My grandmother was a member of Congress and she was in the Indiana General Assembly for several years. I think, throughout the years I served as a precinct committee person, a ward chair, I was a youth activist. In fact, in high school I organized the effort to get the first Black History class put in Manual High School in the early '90s. And so I was an activist from years ago and it was really a calling for me. It was something I had an interest in, the business and the entertainment industry and other things, but it was really a calling for me, seeing a need and filling that need, and so I sat on the city council before coming to Congress, and ever since then, you know, I'm a strong believer in the Golden Rule, and for me it just reinforced the Golden Rule. I felt like politics was a vehicle for me to help others.

Andre Carson said while following in his grandmother's footsteps was a big challenge, there were others along the campaign trail.

Rosemary Pennington: Did you have any worries that being a Muslim was going to be a problem when you began running for office?

AC: I didn't have any worries. I think my concerns were that there are some people who have great bigotries and prejudices against other folk. I think we have a legacy, a dark legacy, of religious bigotry, homophobia, sexism, and racism and the like. And so dealing with these different-isms is always a challenge, but it's also been a great tool to educate people.

RP: Was there ever a point when you were campaigning where your religion turned into more of an issue than perhaps the issues you were running on?

AC: Oh, absolutely, in the initial stages it became an issue. In fact, unfortunately, a few of my opponents were hoping to tap into some fears people have or the lack of knowledge people have in regard to Muslims, but it became a platform once again to show that Muslims are people. Many Muslims care about the country, about the great Hoosier state, about the economy, the foreclosures, and the war in Iraq. At the end of the day, white, black, red, or yellow, it doesn't matter what religion you are. People are concerned about what you are going to do to address their needs.

RP: President Obama, of course, in his inaugural address and in his speech in Cairo and then in his Ramadan address he gave to Muslim communities globally and locally, has been focused on the need to heal the relationship between the United States and Muslims within the country as well as Muslims outside the country. What's been your reaction to the speeches and to these gestures he's been making, and is there more you like to see him do?

AC: Well, you know, I think it's phenomenal, I think it's unprecedented. We just received an invitation to the first Ramadan iftar at the White House under his leadership. I think we have a visionary, universal president who grew up and was raised in Islamic countries and has been exposed to different faith systems and religions, so he has the kind of sensitivity that you really want in a president. I think under the Bush administration you saw this dogmatic, imperialistic regime that was really one-sided and subtly and covertly and overtly promoted this ideology that America is the greatest and only country in the world worth really caring about. And so President Obama, he realizes the importance of having critical relationships with Muslims. I mean, we're talking about nearly two billion people on Planet Earth and, you know, a lot of the natural resources we utilize in this country come from Islamic nations. It's critically important not only to build relationships with people because it's for the greater good of humanity, but building the relationships in our counterterrorist efforts and our efforts to build bridges in our global understanding; it's always good to have friends on all sides of the aisle.

EIGHT

SARAH THOMPSON: WOMEN IN ISLAM, CONVERTING

http://purl.dlib.indiana.edu/iudl/media/930b88rc92

Noblesville, Indiana, native Sarah Thompson converted to Islam when she was in college. This is the story of her experience as a convert.

✦

I feel really blessed because my family reacted better than other families I've heard about. My mom was like, "Okay, great, this is wonderful. What can I do?" And she went out and bought fifteen scarves. She was just, like, amazing.

My parents are divorced, and my dad and my stepdad took it the hardest, I think. My dad really thought he was okay with it, but over time, I think as he realizes other people find out or just how real it is, and the same with my stepdad, I think they had a little difficulty with it. But for the most part all my brothers and sisters are really accepting of it. I definitely lost a lot of friends because of it. They think I'm crazy, but those were friends that weren't meant to be my friends I guess. And those were friends that were peripheral friends. They weren't really good friends anyway. All my good friends, all my family, they've been supportive.

I've always been a really strong feminist, so when I say they thought I was crazy, that's what they meant. You know, they had a very limited idea of what Islam is, and it is the woman in the hijab and it is this woman in a veil that is being oppressed and that sort of the image.

I was at an art exhibit last week and a lot of us were talking about this, and, you know, Islam is a religion that doesn't want to be represented by symbols, and so what happens is the media or whoever is trying to represent us pick something and that sort of becomes the woman in the veil, I guess. And for me, I didn't feel oppressed, but I didn't necessarily feel liberated in Christianity or the life that I was living, and I definitely feel more liberated and more free in Islam.

The way that some women are treated in other countries is cultural and it's definitely not Islamic, and in the Qur'an it says, "Men have this right and women have this right; men have this right and women have this right," and it's the same rights. And so that women should be educated and treated equally. It recognizes that there are differences between men and women and we may have different rules in certain situations, but I think that's something that's just misunderstood. Culturally, maybe people live in a very conservative society and because Islam is a part of your day, it's a part of your life in every sense; it's easy to get it confused with the culture it's a part of.

I didn't necessarily have a near-drowning moment like Cat Stevens, or Yusuf Islam. I was just tired of the way my life was going, and I think what struck me the most was the peacefulness of it. It really is a community religion, but it's also focused on you and your relationship with God and you making your prayers every day and your intent being right every day and basically that only He knows what you've done. You know, on the outside it might look like you're doing something, but maybe it's not for Him or, you know, for other reasons that only He knows. So it was very peaceful to me, the religion, and what people talked about and making the five prayers a day and having this continuous spirituality in your life because of that.

It was more difficult in the beginning, in the sense that I was very worried about what would happen. I was very worried what my family would think or what people would think because it's not really a religion that's thought of being anywhere other than the Middle East and it's so closely linked to terrorism, which is just ridiculous. I was just worried. I was like, oh, I have these friends, I have these family members, what if my family turns against me or something because they are a little more conservative. I had some really, really good friends and they would say, "You just make prayers for these people and if your prayers are pure then God will turn their heart toward you and if they aren't your friends anymore then they weren't meant to be your friends." And it was just basic things that you should know anyway, but at the time you have to be talked out of your sadness. That was life changing. And I think that's the biggest shift that I've made, that in my mind is that rather just saying I'm putting my faith in God to actually do it. And so I would pray every day every prayer to God that they would turn their hearts toward me and every day more and more would turn toward me, so in that sense it's been much easier.

NINE

DAAYIEE ABDULLAH:
BEING OUT AND BEING MUSLIM

http://purl.dlib.indiana.edu/iudl/media/g54x51jm5d

Imam Daayiee Abdullah realized he was gay when he was a teenager, and more than ten years later he also realized he was Muslim. Abdullah grew up in Detroit, Michigan, the son of two highly educated African American parents. Abdullah was encouraged to always be true to himself. When he came out, he says his parents were incredibly supportive.

Abdullah discovered Islam in his late twenties, while a student in China. When he made the decision to become Muslim after returning to the United States, his parents, once again, were supportive. Abdullah is now considered by many in the Muslim LGBT community to be the imam of gay Muslims. This is his story.

❀

To be gay and Muslim, at times, people will say is an oxymoron, but in actuality it's a formulation that shows the diversity within Islam. That people can be a variety of backgrounds. As the Qur'an says to look to the nature of the world, and from that you can see the diversity and understand that Allah's understanding of the world and the universe he's created is full of diversity, but you find the oneness, the unification, of all in those various diverse aspects.

I had come out in my teen years, and through that process of growth, I came out after I graduated from high school. I talked to my parents and explained my circumstance, that I was a homosexual and that was the way I understood the world, my sexual life in terms of that, and my parents were able to understand that. Because I was still young, I received the training they had wanted for their sons. And so I was not any different than my brothers, and so that variance did not cause them any disturbance in their understanding of who I was as a person.

When I was twenty-nine, I went back to school, and a year after entering school I went to Beijing University. I went there for my study abroad, and it was there that I got introduced to Islam. And through that process, I went for *khutba*, the Friday morning *khutba*, and while there the *khutba* was done both in Chinese and in Arabic, and when it was done in Chinese it made perfect sense to me. So it wasn't until a little while later that I actually made my conversion, but that was my real introduction to it. And while there I asked them, "Well, what about being gay and Muslim?" and they didn't find anything wrong with it because in Chinese culture, being gay was not necessarily the norm, but it was something that was understood because of their thousands of years of history. And so within that whole construct of being gay and being Muslim and also of being Chinese, it wasn't considered a negative situation, so it definitely sparked my interest.

The type of reactions I get are varied. There are those who understand the circumstances of a person saying they identify with same-sex orientation, they don't always agree with it. And then that animosity that may be there goes from "you have to be celibate and never do anything in terms of your sexual orientation, playing out a role within it" to the others who felt like if I did do such a thing that they should kill me. So it was this wide expanse. But I found that those individuals who had a negative perspective frequently didn't understand the Qur'an and were following traditional, cultural understandings of what homosexuality was within an Islamic context. There were those who were thinking in a much broader sense, but not necessarily supporting that aspect of it, but were much more lenient in saying, "God may have created you this way, but it's something as a culture and as a religion it's something we understand you should not do." So we had a wide expanse there.

There are times that I have wished that I was not so public. And that makes it difficult sometimes, because there are times I go someplace and people go, "Hey, there's that gay imam," and so I can't step outside of my role a lot of times. But I know that when I asked God for the opportunity to help people, when I started this venture, then God has fulfilled that, so that meant that I had to give up some of those private moments so that I could fulfill it. So I don't feel bad about it, I just know that there are times when I'm like, "Oh, here comes another one." But, needless to say, because of it I find that when I get those e-mails from young people who say, "You know I was contemplating suicide. I was going to throw Islam away" and then they say, "But your words helped me maintain my faith" or "to not take my life" or "to understand that I can be whole as who I am," that's the joy that I get out of it. And I know that if I get an e-mail from one there's another ten who wish they could and another hundred who wish they had nerve enough to do so. So I know that I am influencing people's lives for the better, and the only thing I can do is wait for Allah's judgment to tell me if I'm right or wrong in what I do.

TEN

AZIZ ALQURAINI:
MOSQUES: HOUSES OF PRAYER,
HEARTS OF COMMUNITIES

http://purl.dlib.indiana.edu/iudl/media/791s45rc2t

Virtually anywhere you find a Muslim community, you'll find a mosque, or masjid, its name in Arabic. The masjid is where Muslims gather on Fridays—the holy day—for the congregational prayer as well as for other prayers throughout the week. But a mosque is more than simply a house of worship. It's often the heart of the Muslim community, many offering much more than prayer services. The mosque in Bloomington, Indiana, for instance, offers Arabic lessons on Sundays. It also often has open houses for the community at large to help Muslims and non-Muslims get to know each other.

Aziz Alquraini, journalism student at Indiana University, wanted to show people the multiple facets of mosques, and he created a video about Bloomington's. He talked with Rosemary Pennington about shooting the video as well as what the mosque means to him.

Aziz Alquraini: I'm from Kuwait. I did this video, and I wanted people to know, to inform them about the services the mosque has, beside the praying time. They offer classes for children to teach them Arabic and Qur'an and the Prophet stories, so it's not just about praying. It's about praying and classes.

Rosemary Pennington: Why was it important for you to show people the other things the mosque does?

AA: I had a lot of questions about this issue. People just ask me, "Why do you go to the mosque?" And I said, "I go to prayer and sometimes, also, I teach there. I teach Arabic." You can volunteer to teach Arabic there. So they ask me, "What do you do for weekends?" And I said, "Every Sunday I got to teach in the mosque beside praying."

RP: So how important is the mosque to you, personally, whether it's here or it's back home in Kuwait? How important is it to you?

AA: Back home, you know, Friday is the holy day for Muslims. I mean, it's not the only day that's important, but you can go anytime you feel like you want to pray and anytime you want to meet people, anytime you want to talk there about religion, you know? It's important, I think, for most Muslims here in Bloomington.

RP: So you go to pray but you also go to be involved, it sounds like, in the community as a whole. It's not just about praying it's about meeting the rest of . . .

AA: It's about meeting the rest of the Muslim people here and to introduce myself to work together on events like this weekend; we're making something called "Awareness Panel" for Muslim people and also for other religions, and I think the week after we're doing something about fasting and helping the poor people. We usually do it at Ramadan, but we're doing it next week to inform people about what Ramadan means to us.

RP: Are there many differences between going to mosque back home in Kuwait and going to mosque here?

AA: The only difference I see is the diversity. People from all over. Muslims from all over the world, they come to mosque here, but in Kuwait you just see Kuwaiti people there, that's all. That is the only difference.

RP: This video, was it shown in class, about the Bloomington mosque? Were there many other Muslims in your class?

AA: Actually, I did it with a Muslim student. Her name is Sarah, and I think we were the only Muslims in the class.

RP: If there's one thing that people should know about mosque, about going to mosque or what a mosque means to a Muslim, what do you think it would be?

AA: I want them to think that the mosque is not just, like, a place to pray. It's a place to meet people and introduce them to a religion maybe they don't know about or maybe they don't know a lot about, and maybe learn Arabic there. If they want to learn Arabic they can go to the mosque and there's free classes there.

RP: So, should a non-Muslim feel comfortable going into the mosque?

AA: I've met a lot of Americans. I've seen a lot of Americans there in mosque. They used to go there every Friday since this is the holy day for Muslims to meet the people there and, you know, talk with them and they want to ask something they don't know about.

CRASH COURSE
IN ISLAM

ONE

THE FIVE PILLARS OF ISLAM

http://purl.dlib.indiana.edu/iudl/media/049g15cd65

The Five Pillars of Islam are the foundation of the entire faith. Without the pillars there is no Islam.

The pillars include:

- The profession of faith: There is no God but God, and Muhammad is his messenger. It is considered by many scholars the most important of the five.
- Prayer is also considered a pillar; it is intended to focus a Muslim's mind on Allah and is practiced five times a day.
- The giving of alms, zakat, is another important pillar, although only those who have the means to give must do it.
- Observing the month of Ramadan—in which Muslims fast from sunup to sundown—is the fourth pillar.
- The fifth is the hajj—the once-in-a-lifetime pilgrimage to Mecca Muslims are expected to make if they can afford it.

These five are the most widely observed and recognized pillars of Islam. There are some who think a sixth—jihad—should be added. And there are other groups who think there should be as many as seven, but the majority of Muslims live their lives within the framework of the Five Pillars.

TWO

THE SIX ARTICLES OF FAITH

http://purl.dlib.indiana.edu/iudl/media/079524kt19

You may have heard of the Five Pillars of Islam, but have you heard of the Six Articles of Faith? The Five Pillars of Islam—the profession of faith, prayer, zakat, Ramadan, and the hajj—are considered the foundation of the faith. But the Six Articles are also important. Without them, there is no faith.

To be a Muslim one must believe in all six. A Muslim must believe in the oneness of Allah; God had no parents, siblings, or children. Allah is singular and unique. Another article of faith is the belief in the existence of angels. A Muslim must also have faith in the revelations of God; these include the Qur'an, Torah, and the Gospels. Additionally, Muslims must believe in the prophets, many of whom are responsible for bringing Allah's revelations to man. Among the prophets are the Prophet Muhammad, Jesus, and Moses.

Resurrection and a day of judgment, which are crucial to the Christian faiths, are also crucial to Islam. A Muslim must believe he or she will one day be resurrected and be judged for his or her deeds on earth. The final article of faith is the belief in predestination. A Muslim must believe Allah knows everything, past, present, and future, and that God controls everything that exists and has ever existed.

THREE

THE PROFESSION OF FAITH

http://purl.dlib.indiana.edu/iudl/media/v33r86c83t

In Christian faiths, to become a full-fledged member of the religion, one must be baptized. To become a Muslim, however, a person simply needs to make the profession of faith.

In English the profession of faith is "There is no god but God and Muhammad is his messenger." And while this can be made privately, Muslims believe it's best if the profession of faith is done before witnesses.

When uttering what is called the shahada, a person is stating that, indeed, he or she believes Allah is the only god, that Allah never had a son, and that Allah is indivisible.

The second part of the statement, that Muhammad is Allah's messenger, means that a person is willing to follow the teachings of the Prophet. A Muslim is willing to avoid those things Muhammad said were forbidden and to worship Allah as Muhammad has said to, because the manner of worship was, in fact, revealed to the Prophet by Allah.

Someone who becomes a Muslim is also agreeing to accept the Six Articles of Faith in Islam as well as the Five Pillars of Islam.

FOUR

DO MUSLIMS WORSHIP MUHAMMAD?

http://purl.dlib.indiana.edu/iudl/media/x61d57156w

Many people think Muslims worship Muhammad, but that's not true. Muhammad is not a deity. Instead Muslims believe he is the last in a line of prophets that includes Abraham and Jesus. And like many of his predecessors, Muhammad came to his role reluctantly.

His prophetic nature was revealed by the Angel Gabriel as Muhammad was meditating in a cave not far from Mecca. But Muhammad, at first, refused to believe he could be a prophet. He was a member of the most powerful tribe in Mecca and was a successful businessman. Like many he contemplated the spiritual, but religion was not something he studied closely. Eventually, with the support of his wife, Muhammad accepted his role and began transcribing the Qur'an—the Muslim holy book—as it was revealed to him.

At the same time, Muhammad began to challenge the polytheistic beliefs that abounded in Mecca and the Arabian Peninsula. His new teaching, that there is "No God but God," would help lead the cities of Mecca and Medina to war, with Muhammad and his followers triumphant. With their victory, these first Muslims, with Muhammad as their leader, set up Islam as the dominant faith in the region.

FIVE

THE WILL OF ALLAH

http://purl.dlib.indiana.edu/iudl/media/z902962541

Islam, like some branches of Christianity, adheres to the idea of predestination. For Muslims, Allah knows and sees everything; he knows the outcomes, good or bad. Nothing happens in this world that Allah does not know, that Allah has not permitted.

Even things considered evil are not outside Allah's realm. It is thought that the evils that happen now will eventually result in human good man cannot understand.

But, although God knows all, that does not mean there is no free will in Islam. Muslims believe Allah has written down all things in the Preserved Tablet, and all that happens or will happen is in there. It's there now because God exists outside time. So Allah knows what choices men and women will make, but does not stop them from making them.

Quite often, when Muslims refer to the future, they preface what they say with the phrase "Insha'Allah" or "God willing." It's an acknowledgment that humans do not know what's coming. They can only hope for certain outcomes but, in the end, it all rests in God's hands.

SIX

WHAT IS JIHAD?

http://purl.dlib.indiana.edu/iudl/media/475247fror

Many people outside Islam think they know what jihad means: "holy war," they've been told by pundits or reporters. And, in part, they're right, but that's not the whole story.

Jihad can mean "holy war" or, more correctly, "struggle." That struggle doesn't have to be with those outside Islam. In fact, jihad is something that often focuses Muslims inward.

There are actually two jihads—the lesser and the greater jihad. The lesser jihad is actually the one most people are familiar with, "holy war." But the Qur'an cautions Muslims against fighting unnecessarily. War is to be waged as a defensive measure, not an offensive one.

The more important jihad is the greater jihad. It is an inner struggle for Allah—a struggle to be a better person—in this sense pursuing a degree can be seen as jihad.

But jihad can also be seen as a struggle to improve society. Although Gandhi was not Muslim, his struggle for Indian independence can be considered this kind of jihad. On a religious level, Jihad is an attempt to find harmony among the ideas of submission to Allah, faith, and righteous living.

SEVEN

WHAT IS THE MEANING OF
THE WORD "ISLAM"?

http://purl.dlib.indiana.edu/iudl/media/z70890to72

In Arabic, the word "Islam" means submission or surrender, but it was derived from the root word "salam." From this root word, you can also derive the words "peace" and "safety." Many people feel that Islam implies some sort of enslavement to Allah, but others find it more helpful to define the word "Islam" as surrender.

Many religions have a concept of surrender to God. In Jewish history, after the ancient Hebrews obeyed God's commands, they had a long period of prosperity and stability.

In Christianity, surrendering to God is a way of putting your life into more capable hands; in fact, Jesus asked many of his disciples to surrender their livelihoods and follow him. So, if we look at the word "Islam" in this way, we can understand why obeying Allah's commands and trusting in Allah's wisdom could bring about peace for a Muslim.

The word does not represent a one-sided relationship where the believer is enslaved to Allah. Rather, the word "Islam" indicates a covenant between Allah and his followers, where a Muslim surrenders his or her will to Allah in return for peace or safety.

EIGHT

WHAT IS A FATWA?

http://purl.dlib.indiana.edu/iudl/media/n49to54r4g

You may have heard the term "fatwa" before—especially if you're a fan of writer Salman Rushdie—and you may think a fatwa is a kind of death sentence. Well, it's not.

A fatwa is simply an opinion handed down by an Islamic scholar about some aspect of Islamic law. For Sunni Muslims, a fatwa is a nonbinding opinion. For members of the Shi'a sect, it can be binding depending upon the scholar. And while a fatwa may not necessarily be binding, it can be used by judges when making legal decisions.

Past fatwas have dealt with everything from banning the smoking of cigarettes by Muslims to banning the stockpiling of nuclear weapons by Muslim nations.

Of course, it was media coverage of Rushdie affair of the 1980s—when Iran's Ayatollah Khomeini issued a fatwa saying Rushdie should be put to death for his book *The Satanic Verses*—that the term "fatwa" became synonymous with death sentence. It's a misunderstanding that continues to be perpetuated by many in the media.

NINE

THE QUR'AN:
JUST A BOOK?

http://purl.dlib.indiana.edu/iudl/media/b68x31rk8h

Any book that's believed to hold religious truths is often considered sacred. The Bible and the Jewish Torah are both thought to be inspired by God. For Jews, after a copy of a Torah is blessed, it is a great sin to harm it in any way. Also, many Christians treat the Bible with special care. Similarly, the Qur'an is held in high regard.

Though the Qur'an's teachings have been written down in book form, Muslims consider God to be the true author. It's believed to be a word-for-word transcription of Allah's message to mankind. The bound book—called the mus-Haf—is considered just a vessel in which the sounds reside. The Qur'an, itself, is those sacred sounds.

In fact, for many years it was passed down as an oral text. Muhammad recited it, and devoted Muslims carefully memorized it. To this day, there are still Muslims who memorize the entire Qur'an. For many, the only way to truly learn the Qur'an's teachings is to listen to recitations of it by those who've memorized the text.

TEN

ISHMAEL AND ISLAM

http://purl.dlib.indiana.edu/iudl/media/w62f26996d

In the Old Testament, Abraham cannot have a child with his wife, Sarah. So she gives him her handmaiden Hagar. With Hagar, Abraham has a child, a son, Ishmael. Eventually, though, in her old age, Sarah conceives of a child with divine help. That child is Isaac. After the birth of her son, Sarah forces Abraham to send Hagar and Ishmael away from their home. In the Qur'an, though, it is Allah who tells Abraham to send Hagar and Ishmael into the desert.

While some Jews and Christians believe they are descendants of Isaac, Muslims believe they are the inheritors of Ishmael's legacy, that they, along with Jews and Christians, are the "Children of Abraham."

And they believe it was Ishmael, not Isaac, whom Abraham almost sacrificed to God. The sparing of Ishmael's life is celebrated with the festival Eid ul-Adha. When God spared Ishmael, the boy was replaced with a ram, and it is because of this Muslims make animal sacrifices during the festival.

Ishmael is highly regarded in Islam for his goodness and wisdom. After wandering in the desert with his mother—Hagar's search for water is reenacted during the hajj each year—they settled in Mecca. There it is believed Ishmael built the Ka'aba with Abraham.

ELEVEN

DO MUSLIMS BELIEVE IN JESUS?

http://purl.dlib.indiana.edu/iudl/media/5644753j73

Jesus is a special figure for both Christians and Muslims. Christians view Jesus as the divine son of God and a savior, but in Islam, Jesus is a prophet. Like Muhammad, he is greatly revered as a man who shared a message from Allah with the world.

For Muslims, Jesus is one of many prophets, starting with Adam and ending with Muhammad. But Jesus is still distinct and exceptional in Islam. Muslims believe Jesus was sent directly to the Hebrews, but his teachings reached a more universal audience through the Christian Gospels. Since only a few prophets transmitted sacred texts—Moses, Muhammad, Jesus— these prophets are greatly respected in Islam.

Also, like Christians, Muslims believe that Jesus was formed directly by Allah and placed into Mary's womb. Adam is the only other prophet who is also considered an original creation.

Finally, Muslims believe that Jesus will return to restore justice at the end of time and defeat the unrighteous.

TWELVE

THE CRESCENT MOON AND ISLAM

http://purl.dlib.indiana.edu/iudl/media/237h73qz0p

For many people the image of the crescent moon and Islam go hand-in-hand. The two have become so entwined in the popular imagination that it's led some to believe that Muslims worship a moon god, which isn't true.

Muslims worship Allah, who they believe is also the god of the Jews and Christians. But how did the two, the moon and Islam, become so closely associated? It all goes back to the Ottomans.

The Muslim Ottoman Empire controlled large swaths of the Middle East and North Africa when, as any empire builders, they decided they wanted to expand, and the territory they wanted was in Europe; eventually they would come to control Greece, much of the Balkans, and portions of eastern Europe.

On the Ottoman flag was the crescent moon, a symbol the Turks adopted from the city of Constantinople after conquering it. Because the crescent moon was the symbol for the Ottomans, it also became the symbol for Muslims in general for many in the West.

It has since been adopted by some Muslim nations, finding its way onto the flags of countries as diverse as Malaysia, Pakistan, and Algeria, although some in the Muslim community reject the crescent moon because it can be seen as a pagan symbol.

THIRTEEN

MUSLIM PRAYER:
HOW DO MUSLIMS PRAY?

http://purl.dlib.indiana.edu/iudl/media/j13900q035

Every day millions of Muslims turn toward Mecca and pray. They are required to pray five times a day: at daybreak, noon, midafternoon, sunset, and evening, although there are some Muslims who combine prayers. The prayers are said in Arabic, no matter what the person's native tongue.

Prayer in Islam is ritualized, with some critics saying the ritual takes away from the spiritual. But Muslims don't see it that way. The five prayers, together with the movements involved in them, are designed to combine meditation, devotion, moral elevation, and physical exercise. The prayers can be said together at mosque or alone.

The prayer is begun by saying "Allahu akbar" or "God is most great." Then Muslims recite the first seven verses of chapter 1 of the Qur'an. Before a prayer can be said, though, Muslims must go through a ritual cleansing to ensure they are both physically and spiritually pure before going before Allah.

FOURTEEN

ARE NON-MUSLIMS ALLOWED
TO GO TO MOSQUE?

http://purl.dlib.indiana.edu/iudl/media/029p097b4c

Historically, the Islamic world has been relatively tolerant and accepting of other religions. In the past, however, nonbelievers were usually prohibited from entering mosques.

Today, there are still mosques that prohibit non-Muslims from entering—most of them are in traditional Middle Eastern communities—but there isn't really any standard policy on who is allowed into a mosque.

There are many mosques in Europe and the United States that are open to non-Muslims. But it is important to show proper respect in the mosque. Non-Muslims are still required to dress conservatively or perhaps take off their shoes. Also, you must speak in a low voice. A mosque is considered a holy place and the proper reverence must be shown.

Some mosques will close to non-Muslims during prayer times so that those praying are not distracted.

Many mosques will be very welcoming. Some mosques even host community events or fundraisers, especially during Ramadan or other festivals, that are open to non-Muslims.

FIFTEEN

THE MUSLIM GREETING

http://purl.dlib.indiana.edu/iudl/media/x21t44qx24

If you've ever heard Muslims greet each other, you've probably heard the standard Muslim greeting.

One person says, "Asalaam Alaykum," roughly translated to "Peace be upon you."

And the other person responds with, "Wa'Alaykum Asalaam," which means "And peace be upon you also."

The greeting comes from the Qur'an and is meant to help promote a sense of brotherhood among Muslims and to reflect the peace that should exist between Muslims from all walks of life.

Whether or not these greetings can be used with non-Muslims is up for debate. There are some scholars who say a Muslim should never use them with non-Muslims, while others say the greetings may be used in times of great need or when non-Muslims use them first.

NOTES

PROLOGUE

1. http://bridge.georgetown.edu/new-study-analyzes-media-coverage-of-islam
-over-time/, accessed April 6, 2017.

1. REFLECTING ON MUSLIM VOICES

1. Edward Curtis, *Muslims in America: A Short History* (Oxford: Oxford University Press, 2009).

2. C. Ogan, L. Willnat, R. Pennington, and M. Bashir, "The Rise of Anti-Muslim Prejudice: Media and Islamophobia in Europe and the United States," *International Communication Gazette* 76, no. 1 (2013): 27–46.

2. SHATTERING THE MUSLIM MONOLITH

1. Pew Research Center, Religion and Public Life, "The Future of World Religions: Population Growth Projections, 2010–2025," http://www.pewforum.org/2015/04/02
/religious-projections-2010–2050/.

2. American-Arab Anti-Discrimination Committee, "Facts about Arabs and the Arab World," http://www.adc.org/2009/11/facts-about-arabs-and-the-arab-world/.

3. BBC, "A Guide to Arabic–10 Facts about the Arabic Language," http://www.bbc
.co.uk/languages/other/arabic/guide/facts.shtml.

4. Helen Hatab Samhan, "Who Are Arab Americans?" *Grolier's Multimedia Encyclopedia*, 2001.

5. Arab American Institute, "Demographics," http://www.aaiusa.org
/demographics.

6. Gallup, "Muslim Americans Exemplify Diversity, Potential," http://www.gallup
.com/poll/116260/Muslim-Americans-Exemplify-Diversity-Potential.aspx.

7. Pew Research Center, U.S. Politics & Policy, "Section 1: Demographic Portrait of
Muslim Americans," http://www.people-press.org/2011/08/30/section-1-a
-demographic-portrait-of-muslim-americans/.

8. Jesse Holcomb, "Religion in the News: Islam and Politics Dominate Religion
Coverage in 2011," Pew Research Center, February 23, 2012, http://www.journalism
.org/2012/02/23/religion-news-0/.

9. Michael Honda, "Hearings on Muslim Americans Is Un-American," *San Francisco Chronicle*, February 28, 2011.

10. Brian Bennett and Geraldine Baum, "Rep. Peter King's Hearing on American
Muslims a 'Very Personal' Quest," *Los Angeles Times*, March 10, 2011.

11. Richard Purcell, "ISIS: The State of Terror (Book Review)," *The SAIS Review of
International Affairs*, November 9, 2015.

12. Charles Winter, "ISIS Is Using the Media Against Itself," *The Atlantic*, March 23,
2016.

13. Wired, "Why ISIS Is Winning the Social Media War," https://www.wired.com
/2016/03/isis-winning-social-media-war-heres-beat/.

14. CNN, "French Court Suspends Burkini Ban," http://www.cnn.com/2016/08/26
/europe/france-burkini-ban-court-ruling/.

15. Fatemeh Fakhraie, "The Media Is Obsessed with How Muslim Women Look,"
CNN, August 30, 2010. http://www.cnn.com/2010/OPINION/08/30/muslim.women
.media/.

16. Islamic Research and Information Center, "Sensationalism Veils: The Portrayal
of Muslim Women in Western News Media," June 24, 2014, http://www.iric.org
/DesktopModules/DnnForge%20-%20NewsArticles/Print.aspx?tabid=112
&tabmoduleid=316&articleId=371&moduleId=584&PortalID=0.

17. Arwa Aburawa, "Revisiting *Marie Claire's* Coverage of Muslim Women," *Muslimah Media Watch*, September 20, 2010. http://www.patheos.com/blogs/mmw
/2010/09/finding-a-balance-between-critique-and-praise-revisiting-marie-claires
-coverage-of-muslim-women/.

18. C. Ogan, L. Willnat, R. Pennington, and M. Bashir. "The Rise of Anti-Muslim
Prejudice: Media and Islamophobia in Europe and the United States," *International
Communication Gazette* 76, no. 1 (2013): 27–46.

19. Pew Research Center, Global Attitudes & Trends, "Muslim-Western Tensions
Persist," http://www.pewglobal.org/2011/07/21/muslim-western-tensions-persist/.

20. "Fear Factor: 44 Percent of Americans Queried in Cornell National Poll Favor
Curtailing Some Liberties for Muslim Americans," *Cornell Chronicle*, December 17,

2004, http://www.news.cornell.edu/stories/2004/12/44-americans-favor-curtailing -some-muslim-liberties.

21. Claudia Deane and Darryl Fears, "Negative Perception of Islam Increasing," *Washington Post*, March 9, 2006.

22. Gallup, "Public: Likelihood of Terrorist Attack in United States Now Higher," July 12, 2005, http://www.gallup.com/poll/17245/public-likelihood-terrorist-attack -united-states-now-higher.aspx.

23. Shibley Tehami, "How Trump Changed Americans' Views of Islam—for the Better," *Washington Post Monkey Cage*, January 25, 2017.

24. Brookings Institution, U.S. Foreign Policy, "American Attitudes towards Muslims and Islam," https://www.brookings.edu/research/american-attitudes-toward -muslims-and-islam/.

25. Pew Research Center, Religion & Public Life, "Americans Express Increasingly Warm Feelings Toward Religious Groups," http://www.pewforum.org/2017/02/15 /americans-express-increasingly-warm-feelings-toward-religious-groups/.

26. Society of Professional Journalists, "Muslimedia," http://spj.org/muslimedia.asp.

3. So Near, Yet So Far

1. Project for Excellence in Journalism and the Pew Forum on Religion & Public Life, "Islam and Politics Dominate Religion Coverage in 2011," February 23, 2012, p. 6, http://www.pewforum.org/2012/02/23/religion-in-the-news-islam-and-politics -dominate-religion-coverage-in-2011/.

2. Walter Raleigh, *The Life and Death of Muhomet, the Conquest of Spaine. Together with the Rysing and Ruine of the Sarazen Empire* (London: Daniel Frere, 1637), 6–7.

3. Pew Research Center, "Republicans Prefer Blunt Talk About Islamic Extremism, Democrats Favor Caution," February 3, 2016. http://www.pewforum.org/2016/02/03 /republicans-prefer-blunt-talk-about-islamic-extremism-democrats-favor-caution/, accessed August 24, 2016.

4. Reuters, "How Much of a Threat Does Islam Pose to the United States?" March 27, 2015. http://polling.reuters.com/#!poll/TM514Y15_1, accessed August 24, 2016.

5. Washington Post-ABC News Poll, http://www.washingtonpost.com/wp-srv /politics/polls/postpoll_09072010.html?sid=ST2010090806236, accessed September 26, 2011.

6. Washington Post-ABC News Poll, http://www.washingtonpost.com/wp-srv /politics/polls/postpoll_09072010.html?sid=ST2010090806236, accessed September 26, 2011.

7. Pew Research Center, "U.S. Becoming Less Religious," November 3, 2015, 45. http://www.pewforum.org/files/2015/11/201.11.03_RLS_II_full_report.pdf, accessed August 24, 2016.

8. Margaret Lyons and James Poniewozik, "Where Is God on the Small Screen?" *New York Times*, August 24, 2016, http://www.nytimes.com/2016/08/28/arts/television /greenleaf-oprah-winfrey-transparent-the-path.html, accessed August 23, 2016.

9. Emile Nakhleh, "I Worked in the CIA Under Bush. Obama Is Right to Not Say 'Radical Islam,'" *VOX*, June 28, 2016, http://www.vox.com/2016/6/28/12046626 /phrase-islamic-radicalism-meaningless-counterproductive, accessed August 23, 2016.

10. CNN/ORC poll, February 6, 2012. http://i2.cdn.turner.com/cnn/2012/images /02/16/re12g.pdf, accessed May 5, 2012.

11. Wajahat Ali, Eli Clifton, Matthew Duss, Lee Fang, Scott Keyes, and Faiz Shakir, "Fear Inc.: The Roots of the Islamophobia Network in America," Center for American Progress, August 2011, 16–17, https://www.americanprogress.org/issues/religion /reports/2011/08/26/10165/fear-inc/.

12. Ali et al., 5, 38–41.

13. Alan Gomez, "Poll: Most Say Congressional Hearings on Muslims are OK," *USA Today*, March 10, 2011, http://www.usatoday.com/news/washington/2011-03-09 -muslim-congressional-hearings-poll_N.htm, accessed May 6, 2011.

5. The Prisons of Paradigm

1. Deborah Rodriguez and Kristin Ohlson, *Kabul Beauty School: An American Woman Goes Behind the Veil* (New York: Random House, 2007).

2. Meredith Tax, "NATO Realpolitik and the US Responsibility for Afghan Women," *Guardian*, June 5, 2012. http://www.guardian.co.uk/commentisfree/2012/jun/05 /nato-realpolitik-afghan-women, retrieved February 11, 2013.

3. Laura Bush's address to the nation at http://www.presidency.ucsb.edu/ws/index .php?pid=24992, retrieved February 11, 2013.

4. Tobi Cohen, "Honor Killings on the Rise in Canada," *Vancouver Sun*, June 17, 2010, http://www.vancouversun.com/life/Honour+killings+rise+Canada+Expert /3165638/story.html, retrieved February 11, 2013.

5. "What Happens When We Leave Afghanistan," *TIME*, August 4, 2010, http:// www.time.com/time/covers/0,16641,20100809,00.html, retrieved on February 13, 2013.

6. Unveiling Obsessions

1. Your Veil Is a Battleground, *New York Times Lens Blog*, http://lens.blogs.nytimes .com/2012/05/29/your-veil-is-a-battleground/?_r=0.

2. Newt Gingrich, "No Mosque At Ground Zero," http://humanevents.com/2010 /07/28/no-mosque-at-ground-zero, accessed October 10, 2010.

3. An in-depth investigation by the Center for American Progress Action Fund details the work of a small but well-connected network of experts who spread anti-Islamic

rhetoric to millions of Americans through media partners and grassroots organizations. Blogger Pamela Geller and author Robert Spencer from the Stop Islamization of America (SIOA) are active members of this network, and their Islam bashing reached a climax when they managed to turn the cultural center proposal in New York to the Ground Zero mosque controversy in 2010. For more on the money trail, policy experts, and the media sponsors of this Islamophobia network, read Center for American Progress Action Fund, "Fear, Inc.: The Roots of the Islamophobia Network in America," http://www.americanprogress.org/issues/2011/08/islamophobia.html.

4. Samuel Huntington, *The Clash of Civilizations and the Remaking of World Order* (New York: Simon & Schuster, 2009).

5. For more on this, see Pew Research, "Muslim Americans: Middle Class and Mostly Mainstream," http://pewresearch.org/pubs/483/muslim-americans; and Gallup, "Muslim Americans Exemplify Diversity, Potential," http://www.gallup.com/poll/116260/muslim-americans-exemplify-diversity-potential.aspx.

6. Since 9/11, a new generation of Muslim individuals took to the web to "correct the record" on Islam and highlight the Muslim point of view. This is not an exhaustive list but it is representative of some of the most prominent sites and individuals who are frequently consulted around news about Islam: alt-Muslim (of Shaheed Amanullah), alt-Muslimah, *Muslimah Media Watch, Goatmilk* (blog of Wajahat Ali), Eboo Patel, Irshad Manji, Mona Eltahawy, Asma Uddin, Hamza Yusuf, Zaid Shakir, Reza Aslan, Haroon Moghul, Aziz Poonawalla, Daisy Khan.

7. Muslim Public Affairs Council, "Our Narrative, Our Civic Responsibilities: A Declaration by Young Muslim American Leaders," http://www.mpac.org/programs/young-leaders-development/our-narrative-our-civic-responsibilities.php.

8. Muslim Public Affairs Council, "Our Narrative, Our Civic Responsibilities."

9. *All-American Muslim* aired on TLC in November 2012 and featured five Arab American Muslim families from Dearborn, Michigan. The show debuted to a strong 1.7 million viewers but was unable to retain the same ratings throughout its short run. *All-American Muslim* was canceled amid concerns by some major advertisers about its edgy content. The home improvement retail store Lowe's pulled its ads allegedly after an evangelical organization in Florida complained about the show and its whitewashing of violent Islam.

10. Comedian Shazia Mirza has performed in many cities in Europe and the United States. She often criticized the ethnic label attached to her comedy in her shows. For more on this, see Kiran Bharthapudi, "British Muslim Takes Laughs to the US," *BBC News*, http://news.bbc.co.uk/2/hi/south_asia/4803044.stm.

11. Stuart Hall, "New Ethnicities," in *Black Film, British Cinema*, ed. Kobena Mercer (London: Institute of Contemporary Arts, 1988).

12. Hall, "New Ethnicities," 27.

13. Hall, "New Ethnicities," 28.

7. How Does the British Press Represent British Muslims?

1. This chapter is based on the author's previous article published originally in the *Global Media Journal—Canadian Edition*, in 2011, vol. 4, iss. 2 under the title "Change and Continuity in the Representation of British Muslims Before and After 9/11: The UK Context," at http://www.gmj.uottawa.ca/1102/v4i2_poole.pdf.

2. D. Deacon, J. Downey, E. Harmer, J. Stanyer, and D. Wring, "The Narrow Agenda: How the News Media Covered the Referendum," in *EU Referendum Analysis 2016: Media, Voters and the Campaign: Early Reflections from Leading UK Academics*, ed. D. Jackson, E. Thorsen, and D. Wring (The Centre for the Study of Journalism, Culture and Community Bournemouth University, 2016).

3. T. Modood, "Between Nationalism and Civilizationism: The European Populist Moment in Comparative Perspective," *Ethnic and Racial Studies* (2017): 1–36, http://dx.doi.org/10.1080/01419870.2017.1294700.

4. J. Martin, "The Rhetoric of Excess," in *EU Referendum Analysis 2016: Media, Voters and the Campaign: Early Reflections from Leading UK Academics*, ed. D. Jackson, E. Thorsen, and D. Wring (The Centre for the Study of Journalism, Culture and Community Bournemouth University, 2016).

5. *The Satanic Verses* (1989), written by Indian-British author Salman Rushdie, was interpreted by some as being blasphemous against Islam. It led to an international outcry and a "fatwa," issued by Iran's Ayatollah Khomeini, on Rushdie. It is widely considered as the catalyst for the demonization of Muslims in the UK.

6. Fred Halliday, *Islam and the Myth of Confrontation: Religion and Politics in the Middle East* (London: I. B. Tauris, 1996).

7. To avoid a reductive, simplistic analysis I sought to examine a particular context (the UK) and media form (the press) to demonstrate how discourse both constructs and is a construct of political life and social relations (ideas about Muslims are both fed into the media by wider society but are also constructed by them).

8. Elizabeth Poole, *Reporting Islam: Media Representations of British Muslims* (London: I. B. Tauris, 2002). The study used both quantitative and qualitative methods. The press in the UK is largely conservative excluding the *Guardian*, which has a liberal bias.

9. John E. Richardson, *(Mis)Representing Islam: The Racism and Rhetoric of British Broadsheet Newspapers* (Amsterdam: John Benjamins Publishing Company, 2004).

10. Kerry Moore, Paul Mason, and Jerry Lewis, *Images of Islam in the UK: The Representation of British Muslims in the National Print News Media 2000–2008*, 2008. Report published by Cardiff School of Journalism, Media and Cultural Studies commissioned by Channel 4.

11. For example, in 1994 the *Times* ran just over 80 stories on British Islam compared to nearly 160 in the *Guardian*, but by 2003 the ratio was 388:314 (Poole, *Reporting Islam*; Poole, *The Effects of September 11*).

12. Poole, *Reporting Islam*.

13. See Poole, *Reporting Islam*; Poole, *The Effects of September 11*; Mark Featherstone, Siobhan Holohan, and Elizabeth Poole, "Discourses of the War on Terror: Constructions of the Islamic Other in the Wake of 7/7," *International Journal of Media and Cultural Politics* 6, no. 2 (2010): 169–86; and Kim Knott, Elizabeth Poole, and Teemu Taira, *Media Portrayals of Religion and the Secular Sacred* (Farnham: Ashgate, 2013).

14. Poole, *Reporting Islam*.

15. Moore, Mason, and Lewis, *Images of Islam in the UK*.

16. Richardson, *(Mis)Representing Islam*.

17. Poole, *Reporting Islam*.

18. *Times*, October 17, 2008, 24–25.

19. *Times*, October 16, 2008, 3.

20. *Times*, October 10, 2008, 22–23.

21. *Times*, October 10, 2008, p. 22–23.

22. Sean O'Neill, "Deadly Loners Who Don't Show on the Radar," *Times*, October 16, 2008, 3.

23. *Sun*, October 6, 2008, 25.

24. Christine Savage, Letter, *Sun*, October 24, 2008, 47.

25. "The X Fatwa," *Sun*, October 21, 2008, 1 and 5.

26. Elizabeth Poole, "'Muslim Media' and the Politics of Representation: Media and Cultural Responses to Diversity Issues in Britain," *Middle Eastern Journal of Communication and Culture* 7, no. 1, 101–18.

27. Arun Kundnani, *The End of Tolerance: Racism in 21st Century Britain* (Ann Arbor: Pluto Press, 2007).

11. New Media and Muslim Voices

1. Umberto Eco, *Inventing the Enemy: Essays* (New York: Houghton Mifflin, 2011); Shani Orgad, *Media Representation and the Global Imagination* (Malden, MA: Polity Press, 2012).

2. Benedict Anderson, *Imagined Communities: Reflections on the Origin and Spread of Nationalism* (New York: Verso, 1983).

3. Linda Woodhead, "Old, New and Emerging Paradigms in the Sociological Study of Religion," *Nordic Journal of Religion and Society* 2, no. 22 (2009): 103–21.

4. Lily Kong, "Mapping 'New' Geographies of Religion: Politics and Poetics in Modernity," *Progress in Human Geography* 25, no. 2: 211–33.

5. Nabil Echchaibi, "From Audiotapes to Videoblogs: The Declocalization of Authority in Islam," *Nations and Nationalism* 17, no. 1 (2011): 1–20.

6. Saminaz Zaman, "From Imam to Cyber-Mufti: Consuming Identity in Muslim America," *Muslim World* 98 (2008): 466.

7. Daniel Martin Varisco, "Muslims and the Media in the Blogosphere," *Contemporary Islam* 4, no. 1 (2010): 157–77.

8. danah boyd and Nancy Ellison, "Social Network Sites: Definition, History, and Scholarship," *Journal of Computer-Mediated Communication* 13 (2008): 211.

9. Andrew Hoskins and Ben O'Loughlin, "Media and the Myth of Radicalization," *Media, War, & Conflict* 2, no. 2 (2009): 109.

10. Peter R. Neumann, "The Trouble with Radicalization," *International Affairs* 89, no. 4 (2013): 873–93.

11. Neumann, "The Trouble with Radicalization," 873–93.

12. Shadi Hamid, "Radicalization after the Arab Spring: Lessons from Tunisia and Egypt," December 1, 2015, *Brookings Institution*, https://www.brookings.edu/research/radicalization-after-the-arab-spring-lessons-from-tunisia-and-egypt/.

13. See SPJ Code of Ethics: http://www.spj.org/ethicscode.asp.

14. Michael Schudson, "What's Unusual about Covering Politics as Usual?" in *Journalism After September 11*, ed. B. Zelizer and S. Allan (New York: Routledge, 2002), 43.

INDEX

CPSIA information can be obtained
at www.ICGtesting.com
Printed in the USA
BVOW06s1929200118
505862BV00001B/1/P